INSECURE IN LOVE

HOW TO DOMINATE YOURSELF IN LOVE TO OVERCOME THE FEAR OF ABANDONMENT, ANXIOUS ATTACHMENT, SAVE YOUR CODEPENDENT RELATIONSHIP AND STOP CONTROLLING OTHERS.

A.P. COLLINS

Introduction

Whether you are struggling with insecurities, or you are trying to understand your loved one and help him with his battle, you purchased this book and it will set you on a good path to save your relationship.

Insecurities are triggered by actions and will produce powerful and painful emotions. These emotions decide how we behave, and behavior is one of the elements that influences a relationship. You want to build a strong, healthy relationship but your insecurities and behaviors won't let you. To win the battle with your insecurities you need to understand them. Even if you are trying to help your partner, the best possible thing you can do is show some understanding. This book will offer you clarification; you will recognize certain aspects described here, either in yourself or in your partner. By recognizing, you will acknowledge them, learn how to manage them, and you will be able to build the relationship you want.

This book will help you understand that there is no one to blame for your insecurities. They come naturally, and they depend on your past. They are triggered by actions or experiences, and even though you can't get rid of them, you will learn how to manage them and how to respond to them. This will give you a good start to achieve happiness in your relationship.

In this book, we will explore what love is and why we feel the way we feel about our partner. It will give you understanding and insight into your relationship. You will understand where the problem lies, and it will motivate you to continue fighting for it.

We will also explore insecurities and see how they affect a relationship. Insecurities affect our partners too, and we may be hurting them while trying to deal with our own insecurities. It is important to keep that in mind, after all, we do want to change so we can make our partner happy. You will also see possible sources of insecurity that will encourage you to explore your past. This book will give you some exercises that will teach you how to behave when your insecurities are triggered.

Next, you will go down the path of learning how to manage your emotions, how to stop criticizing yourself and how to deal with constant negative thoughts that keep popping into your mind. Jealousy plays a large part in any couple's lives and this book will offer ways to deal with it. It will also offer you knowledge about the modern, digital age and how it influences our insecurities.

In addition, this book will offer comfort and motivation to continue to build your relationship through chapters about communication and all the other healthy ingredients needed for a strong and happy relationship.

Be prepared to work; dealing with insecurities is not an easy task. It is a journey and be aware it might take some time for you to reach the finish line. You will feel challenged, and you will feel like there is no point in making the effort, but you have to be strong. As you read this book, try keeping a journal of your own thoughts, write down things you recognize in yourself or your partner. Writing is a good way of staying focused and motivated for the work you will have to endure. It will also keep your thoughts in one place so it will be easy for you to reflect on them, notice any patterns that need to be broken, and remind you of your core values.

You can even chart your own progress.

Just the act of buying this book shows you are serious and you do want to change. You want to save your relationship. Congratulations on the courage. It is a brave act to admit to yourself that your relationship might have a problem. Start learning how to deal with insecurities in your relationship right away.

Chapter 1: What Does it Mean to Truly Love?

Love, the topic that baffled the minds of famous artists, poets, writers and even great philosophers like Plato, who were trying to answer what love truly means. In Plato's *Symposium,* there is a great dialog by Aristophanes that describes love as the constant search for the other half of ourselves. Ancient Greeks believed that all humans used to have two faces, four arms and four legs, and all humans were hermaphrodites. Zeus was angry because of their pride and he decided to cut them in half, thus dividing them into a male and a female. Since that day, humans have this unexplainable urge to find the other half that will fill the emptiness they feel and make them whole again. It is believed that in this kind of reunification with our other half, we will know the meaning of true love.

Of course, we are not supposed to believe in this story as a fact; however, its symbolic value is clear and obvious. The concept of soul mates exists in all cultures, as the two sides of the same coin, or simply as destiny. The truth may not be as romantic and mysterious as any ancient stories you might read. Humans are social beings, and we indeed need other people around us to feel complete. However, sometimes just one perfect human is enough to make us feel whole and happy for the rest of our lives. This somewhat romantic view, mixed with attraction, affection and even lust, form a good basis for what is perceived as true love.

No one can claim they are experts in love simply because no one can agree on the definite answer to what love is. One person's "I love you" may mean entirely something else to another. Some people claim they know the "real" answer, but that answer comes from their personal experience and may not apply to yours. Love is completely individual and you need to learn to recognize it in yourself.

If you take a look at all the literature, art, and philosophical works throughout history you will notice a constant debate over what love really is. Is it a choice? Do we get to choose who we love or is it forced on us by social norms? Is it an uncontrollable feeling that floods us, or is it more like the calm waters that carry us to safety? Different cultures and different religions have different answers, but what really matters is your personal experience.

Scientists have tried to do their part and give us an answer to what love is. According to many of them, it is nothing other than a chemical reaction in our bodies that will ensure the procreation and continuation of our species. We choose our partners based on the traits we see in them and we want them to be passed on to our offspring. That's why some people are attracted to intelligence more than physical attractiveness and vice versa. Some people will even go further and choose to produce offspring with one person but spend life with another because he or she is more capable to ensure a comfortable environment suited for growth. Keep in mind that this is not the conscious part of the brain that is making these choices. They are, in fact, instincts, and we call them parental instincts. It is pure biology, which means we could even say we are programed to behave this way and it is not to be seen as a fault or something bad. It is nature, and what is more natural than love?

There are three systems or phases of love that people go through to ensure offspring, and most of the time we aren't even aware of them:

1. **The sex drive or lust**: It evolved in humans and some animals as an instinct that allows us to seek procreation. The sex drive is there to ensure new generations of offspring. Keep in mind that it's also normal to feel lust for someone you are not in love with. Why? We instinctively seek to choose good genes to be passed on to our children. This is how we feel attraction to a certain type of people, people we wouldn't even consider good life partners. However, lust sometimes isn't focused on a particular person. It is within us as a biological need to have children. We will feel it before we even have a potential target. It is truly amazing how nature programmed us, and we might think we are evolved enough to control these urges and instincts, however, they are there whether we like it or not and we cannot easily control them. Whether we choose to ignore them does not diminish their existence and meaning.

2. **Romantic Love**: It is believed it evolved to make sure you focus your mating energy on just one person. We feel it as an obsessive thought toward a person we see as a potential mate. We are even able to shut the entire world out and spend time only with this one person. Our sex drive is increased during this phase and is focused on our partner, and it feels like energy radiating from him or her more than being our own.

3. **Attachment**: It evolved to enable us to remain in union with one partner and guarantee the wellbeing of the resulting offspring. We might choose a partner who has excellent parenting skills and we

might not care about the genes that parents will pass on. It might be a person who doesn't share any genes with the child. As long as he or she is a good provider and cares for you and the child, this is the person you will develop a deep attachment to and who you will trust the most. This is the person you will share your life with, and this connection and deep attachment will often last much longer than the need to provide for the child.

Even those who consciously make a decision not to have children will go through all of these phases. They are biological instincts and no one is immune to them. It happens to everyone, unrelated to gender or social structure. However, some learned behaviors may have an influence on them with more or less success. For example, religion may dictate a person not to act upon his sex drive. In another example, we have arranged marriages in some cultures where we don't choose our life partner out of our free will. This does not make them a worse or a better choice. No matter what restrictions we put on these systems of love, they will exist and we will still feel them.

Some neuroscientists agree that love is a form of addiction. When in love, a person acts much like a drug addict. The constant need to be with the loved one, the feeling of anxiousness when separated, the almost urge to do anything to be in proximity. It is like thirst or hunger. We will do anything to be noticed, loved, and cared for by the object of our attraction. The only difference is that love, especially romantic love, is a natural addiction and as such we recognize it in us and can control it to some extent. People around us will notice we are in love. They can see it by watching our behavior. We might stop eating, have trouble concentrating or listening to other people. We are constantly with our "head in the clouds," thinking of that one person.

There is a difference between the initial feeling of being in love and the attachment we develop for one person over time. The initial burst of love and euphoria may last anywhere between six months to two years and is considered the "honeymoon" phase. Everything is perfect, you feel obsessed with one person and cannot stop thinking about him. The craving for that particular person feels almost comparable to physical pain. The attachment is more like a feeling of a deep connection with someone, the union with a partner in a long relationship.

Science observes that long-term attachment is a drive to spend time with a partner who will care and provide for children. But people stay together long after the children grow out of the need to be cared for. Many cultures, religions, and scientists will agree that this is the time when true love is mature and in its full potential. This is when we see what is common to all these cultures, religions, and philosophies: an attempt to answer what love is. We notice that partners care for one another more than for themselves, and they can be themselves without judging their loved ones. They are capable of accepting each other for who they are.

We could say that love is as important as understanding the meaning of life. Love is the meaning of life. It encourages us to live with full potential. It allows us to give ourselves completely and unconditionally to someone else and not be afraid of being hurt. Love makes us care about another person so much more than for our own lives, and that brings happiness.

We trust our partner completely, and we are capable of showing our most intimate selves to them.

Love does affect our physical and psychological health, and to function as humans we need to take care of both.

Influence of love on physical health: Unreturned love can make us feel sick. We stop eating or increase the amount of food we consume (comfort food). Our immune system suffers, and we are prone to disease. Scientists warn that love can literally break a heart. This is known as Takotsubo cardiomyopathy or broken heart syndrome. The symptoms are very similar to a heart attack: shortness of breath, nausea, and chest pains that follow emotional events such as a break-up or death of a loved one. If you recognize these symptoms in yourself or someone else, talk to professionals. There are cases of people dying due to broken heart syndrome.

But not all effects of love on our health are bad. Love is also known to improve our immune system, lower blood pressure, and it can help us fight anxiety and depression caused by pain or serious disease, thus improving our chances of fighting them. Love is responsible for releasing oxytocin, better known as the "cuddle chemical." This hormone is released when we feel the touch of a loved one, or a kiss, even when we look upon our partner's face. Oxytocin is a hormone that helps us fight physical pain and increases our energy. This is why people "glow" when they are in love or pregnant. This hormone also makes them have a positive view on life and just be more upbeat.

Influence of love on psychological health: Love can both cause and cure anxiety as well as depression. It depends if the love flows both ways. Both depression and anxiety are closely related to feelings of loneliness. If not caused by loneliness, they cause isolation and estrange ourselves from others. Being in a relationship means we have a partner who will share our life with us. Our wishes, dreams, and fears will be acknowledged and we will not feel hopeless. We will cope better with our mental challenges from being able to feel the support of our partner. Those satisfied with their relationship are prone to show lower levels of depression over a short period. Feeling safe and secure in the knowledge that our loved one will always be there for us lowers symptoms of anxiety. The potential for the support and encouragement of a life partner to cure mental illnesses is very real and medicine is paying attention to the beneficial aspects of love.

One could say that science, philosophy, religion and different cultures agree that certain aspects of love are recognized everywhere including feelings of safety, happiness, and intimacy. These may as well be crucial for healthy relationships filled with mutual respect and love. But sometimes one or more of these aspects are missing or are suppressed by one or both partners. This is how we develop unhealthy relationships that might feel like they are doomed to fail. Healthy relationship needs constant work. A happy love life will depend on our acknowledgment of errors and imperfections, and our ability to deal with them. Communication, compassion, and being able to make compromises may be crucial for a healthy long-lasting relationship.

Chapter 2: Insecurity and Its Influence on Relationship

What is Insecurity

Insecurity is the tendency to lack any feeling of confidence or certainty in oneself. We all feel insecure at one time or another. Insecurity can be attached to all aspects of life. The most common insecurities we have are about our looks, jobs, and love life. Most people are capable of resolving their insecurity before it leaves a deeper impact in their lives. Some go through therapy, others can recognize it and deal with it on their own, but many people won't recognize insecurity and will confuse it with other negative feelings, such as jealousy. Helplessness and inadequacy are common feelings for insecure people. Because of these feelings, they are incapable of attending to common daily tasks or even form long-lasting, healthy relationships. People who feel insecure will often lack the ability to fit in society and think their actions and thoughts are constantly being judged by peers. They also believe they aren't worthy of acceptance or success. These beliefs will stop them from trying to achieve more. They will often be stuck in unsatisfying job positions without any motivation to go forward and work on receiving a promotion. They will lack the will to learn, work on themselves, thinking that there is no point as they will never be good enough. Even their love life suffers, probably the most. An insecure person will constantly crave a partner's validation. When he gets it, he will choose not to believe it or believe it's sincere.

The basis of all insecurities is fear. Fear from abandonment, betrayal, and fear of not being good enough. Because of this fear, insecure people have trouble showing and sharing their emotions. Negative reaction on a person's emotions will make them distance themselves even more, and they will fall into loneliness and depression.

Insecurity can be detected by other people no matter how well one thinks he is hiding it. The body language of an insecure person is recognizably different. It expresses confusion, excessive shyness, and fear of maintaining eye contact. Insecure people will often lie about who they are, and what they feel or think. They are more likely to agree with other people's opinions than express their own. Insecure people will refuse to accept compliments, as they believe they do not deserve them. They will often shrug and try to look smaller than they physically are in an attempt to hide themselves from what they believe is constant judgement. In some more serious cases of insecurity, people will act on their bad habits, trying to convince other people how they are not worthy. They will act stupid, rude, or try to put themselves down in any possible way.

Opposite of insecurity is confidence, and many people feel that confidence is the most desirable trait to seek in potential partners. Confidence also means success in a career, in school or love life. If confidence is the most wanted trait, imagine how insecurity must be unattractive. Insecurity is unattractive even to deeply insecure people. It is similar to looking into a mirror and feeling all negative emotions flowing from both sides. Insecure people like confident ones too. But one confident partner will not be able to hold the relationship together alone. His confidence will suffer under the pressure coming from someone who's insecure. The relationship is not healthy, but it may not be doomed to failure. Recognized on time and properly treated, insecurity can be beaten. But to do so, we must fully understand all the dark corners of insecurity, understand what it is doing to your relationship and how it affects you and your partner.

Insecurity in Relationships

In a small amount, insecurity in a relationship can be good as it gets you to work harder and devote yourself more to that relationship. Small jealousy acts can be seen as sweet and make us value our partner more. But the trick is in the small amount of insecurity, if it grows to be pathological, it will most certainly influence the relationship in the most negative way. It will, if not treated, eventually lead to a break-up. The destruction of a relationship caused by one person's insecurities is always very dramatic and painful for both sides. It will leave marks on both partners, deepening insecurities that already exist, or creating other anxieties related to relationships.

Knowing how your insecurities influence the relationship is important. By recognizing the signs of disaster your insecurity is creating, you will acknowledge its existence and can start working on yourself.

We all cope with negative thoughts about our relationships from time to time, and that's normal. We are all somewhat possessive of our partners. It gets really tricky when we start to act on those negative thoughts; when we manifest negative thoughts into negative actions. This is what ruins most relationships. This usually doesn't happen overnight, it takes time and it happens in stages. This is why it's hard for people to recognize the actions of their insecurities.

One of the first signs of insecurities working their way into your relationship is sudden lack of trust. All healthy relationships include mutual trust between partners. Although telling the truth is important, it doesn't mean it's the only aspect of trust. When I say trust, I mean being able to rely on your partner, thinking of him or her as a responsible person who you can completely depend. If you lack trust in your partner, it means you are unable to completely open yourself emotionally. This could stagnate your relationship. Without showing how you feel, or how you think, your relationship will never progress from the early stages and this will only cause more anxiety. Relationships are meant to move forward, and to gain complete trust so your partner becomes the pivotal figure in your life who will always stand by you. Trust also means feeling completely safe in your partner's company. If you don't feel safe, and lack of trust is caused by you being hurt or belittled, it means you are in an abusive relationship and it has nothing to do with your insecurity. We do not give our trust blindly. It has to be earned.

An insecure person will always compare himself to others. In a relationship, this might mean comparing yourself to your partner's exes. It is completely normal to be curious about your partner's previous relationships. After all, we want to know what made our loved one happy in the past, or even what ruined those relationships so we do not make the same mistakes. An insecure person will try to measure up to the relationship a partner previously had, believing that he or she will never be good enough. Constant thinking that your partner's ex is somehow better than you can damage the relationship. Because of the obsession to compare yourself with someone else, you will never be able to show who you are. You will try to act as others, think like others, and imitate others. This will not be the person your partner fell in love with. Simply put, you might not recognize yourself. This is an easy way to lose all that is you. If there is anyone you should be comparing yourself to, it should be future you, the best version of you. This will motivate you to work on yourself and to learn. This will make you a successful, healthy person as long as your goals are within reason.

The constant need for reassurance is another sign of pathological insecurity in a relationship. If you expect your partner to reassure your every decision and action, it can mean you're insecure. You don't trust yourself to make the right decisions. Insecure people mostly seek reassurance that their partner loves them. They will ask numerous times, but the feeling of security will never come. This is because an insecure person is unable to feel self-love. If you think you are unworthy of your love, how do you expect others to love you? And it will not stop with love. Soon enough, you will depend on your partner so much that you will need his or her reassurance in all aspects of your life. Did I make the right decision? Am I doing my job well? Do I look good enough? These are some of the many questions you will ask and expect your partner to give positive answers to all of them so you can feel secure enough to continue with your day.

When it comes to loving yourself, it cannot be achieved without accepting what and who you are. An insecure person will never feel good enough at anything. This might be because their expectations are too high. Or maybe someone else, such as a parent, had expectations that the person in question didn't fulfill. An insecure person often feels pressure to be better, not realizing that better is not always possible. Therefore, they will constantly need the partner's approval that will make them feel good about themselves. You will never manage to be happy if you constantly have doubts about your abilities. For insecure people, hearing reassurances and approvals once is not enough. The doubt is eating at their consciousness, and they start to ask illogical questions such as: "If he can love me like this, who's to say he doesn't love someone else even more?" or "I'm not funny enough. What if he finds someone else who will satisfy his need for laughter?" Questions like these are constantly on the mind of an insecure person. It's a very difficult way of living, and this is why insecurity is, in most cases, followed by depression or some other kind of anxiety. When we accept our limits, our possibilities to which we can rise, we will accept ourselves and rediscover who we are. Only then will we be able to improve, learn more, change and love ourselves.

Another thing that insecure people do so often is overthink. Because of insecurity in their decisions, everything needs to be analyzed and reanalyzed. This goes for partners too. Did he mean what he said? Does she think I'm attractive enough? This is again about reassurance and truth. Insecure people will not trust their partner's words, thoughts, and actions. They will doubt everything their loved one is doing and will overthink what is the real meaning or intention behind the partner's actions. It becomes difficult if you read into your partner's words in a way that will reinforce your insecurities. If you are insecure about your partner's faithfulness, you will spend all of your time and energy into proving that he or she is cheating, you will search all possible clues, you will read into everything they say and you will ask illogical questions. There will be no time or energy left to truly enjoy time spent with your partner, and you will never be able to develop a better relationship.

Everyone has insecurities to some extent, and there is no such thing as a perfectly secure relationship. We mentioned earlier that it's normal and even perceived as sweet to be a little insecure. What really makes a difference between a small healthy dose of insecurity, and large, relationship-breaking pathological insecurity is the way how you handle these situations. First relationships are always filled with insecurities, and this is normal. But if you drag all your insecurities from one relationship to another, the problem might be deeper, and you might require outside help to deal with them. The problem might lie in the way you attach yourself to your new partner or some previous experience you had. Fear plays a big role in relationship insecurity; fear we have from previous experiences, which may or may not be related to our previous love lives.

Chapter 3: The Source of Insecurity

To start feeling better and get rid of the awful sentiment of insecurity, we must find the reason for its existence. Insecurities don't just happen. They can be triggered by past events or traumas. They can be buried so deep within us that we might not have a memory of it. Understanding where it comes from is the first step in beating it.

No matter what aspect of your life makes you feel insecure, the cause for it might come as a surprise. Many who feel insecure about their looks will find the root of the problem is from their childhood, and their parents' desire for a child's success. Parents may push their children toward unrealistic goals, and the child will develop anxiety and insecurity about his possibilities. This will reflect on something as simple as the way he sees himself, how he feels in his own body and his need for his parents' approval.

The same applies to relationships. The source of insecurity in love might be in some traumatic childhood event. Children who witnessed the toxic relationship of their parents might develop insecurities about relationships in general. Or a child who witnessed adultery might grow up to be insecure in his partner's faithfulness. This is how we reflect past events and let them influence our present, even destroy our possible future. To recognize where insecurity comes from, we must dig deep in our experiences and search for possible causes. People will often need help in this search from a therapist or simply someone they can trust to guide them through the memories and emotions related to them.

Insecurity can also be based on recent rejections and failures. People who are already insecure, have low self-esteem and are likely to take rejection and failure more negatively. The feeling of rejection will stay longer with these people, deepening their insecurity. Rejection can reignite old negative feelings and will come as confirmation of his inadequacy. After rejection or failure, people tend to retreat, closing their emotions even more. They will take no comfort offered by friends. They will see it more as an acknowledgment of their nonexistent worthiness, which will enable them to feel even more insecure. Often, rejection will influence other aspects of life and deeply insecure people might not be able to push through the day, their job, or their friendships. If you are rejected, or you are facing recent failures, an important thing to do is give yourself time to heal, and don't close yourself in your house. Get out there, reach out to your friends for support and activate yourself with hobbies and interests.

Insecurity can also be triggered by the tragic events in the past. Events such as the death of a significant other or family member, physical and emotional abuse, threats, broken promises or any other emotional losses that a person has no control will influence us in the most stressful ways. The important thing is to have someone close and supportive to help you get through these stressful events. A child needs nurturing and an understanding caretaker to help develop the needed coping skills. The lack of help, support and feeling of safety will leave deep marks on a person, especially during the vulnerable times of growing up. These marks will leave us vulnerable in future events of loss, and we won't know how to deal with stressful situations.

Attachment

From the moment we are born, we have an instinctive need to attach to our caregivers. This is because infants need their parents or caregivers for survival. We start to develop our attachment systems, and outside factors will influence how we develop these systems.

In the 50s, some psychologists suggested that if we want our children to grow up healthy and develop in the best possible way, a loving and nurturing environment is needed, and a primary caregiver who will be the attachment figure needs to be emotionally open and warm. During that time, this was contradicting everything that was considered good parenting. People used to believe that a firm, objective guiding hand kept at a distance, would make our children develop into strong independent individuals who won't need to rely on anyone for safety.

Children who are deprived of love and emotional stability, and without someone they can develop a bond with, will grow up unable to have a healthy attachment system and will be too needy, insecure, and possessive. The way our caregivers respond to our infantile attachments will determine our future ability to bond, to love, and to care for others. A person who wasn't in a loving environment with a healthy attachment figure will be unable to emotionally open to his partner and will depend too much on their relationship.

Secured Attachment System

Whenever you feel threatened, anxious or upset, your attachment system will turn on. This may be a feeling of longing for home, needing our loved ones immediately, or needing reassurance. In a healthy individual, once the reassurance is found, and the feeling of security returns, attachment systems will shut off. The feeling of calm and comfort are once again present. The secure attachment system comes from our parents' ability to comfort us when we are hurt or ill. Besides comfort, we also need to receive security and emotional availability that we translate into love.

People who grow up with this healthy attachment system provided by their family will have similar habits when it comes to romantic relationships. In a time of need, when we feel insecure and threatened, we will turn to our partner for reassurance and comfort. Once found (provided that the relationship is a healthy one) attachment systems will turn off and we will feel loved and reassured, and we can return the same care to our partner.

Insecure Attachment System

What happens when a person grows up without an attachment figure who is capable of providing a loving, nurturing environment? Once the attachment system is turned on, and a person receives reassurance of a loved one but is unable to feel comforted and safe, they will have an insecure attachment and we can say the system isn't working properly. People like this will have their attachment system constantly on, seeking reassurance for every situation in their life. They will be too needy, too possessive and too dependent on their partner. They will also be unable to open emotionally and develop a relationship with a loved one.

The insecure attachment comes from our own sense of how worthy of love we are. It's only natural to fear rejection if you are not capable of seeing yourself as worthy of love. In psychology this is called *attachment-related anxiety,* and it may come as a feeling of nervousness, loneliness or depression.

This is divided into four main styles of attachment found in adults: *Secure, Anxious-preoccupied, Dismissive-avoidant* and *Fearful-avoidant.* We will discuss each separately later in this chapter.

Ambivalent Attachment System

This attachment system develops early in our childhood when our primary caregiver is inconsistent with devotion, love, and the ability to make the child feel safe. It might be a parent who is often not home in situations when the child needs reassurance, a parent who works too much, or a parent with mental health issues. This creates a chaotic environment for a child to grow up in. This environment is the perfect atmosphere for developing anxieties, anger, insecurity and even hatred toward a parent or a caregiver.

A person who grows up without constant security will have difficulty with attachment. They will seem too chaotic, with an explosive temperament that will often create problems in relationships. The partner will feel confused and unsure how to behave or even help the person in need. People who develop an ambivalent attachment style will demand constant attention but will give nothing in return and he will keep to himself, unable to open emotionally and unable to communicate properly.

Four Attachment Styles in Adults

Secure attachment style: Demonstrated when a person has a positive image of himself and of others. People with a secure attachment style find it easy to emotionally connect with others and they are comfortable showing their emotions. They are able to depend on their partners and let their partners depend on them. They are able to be independent and also seek reassurance in healthy ways when needed. They were raised in a warm and loving environment with healthy attachment figures. This is healthy and is a trait found in most of the adult population.

Anxious-preoccupied attachment style: This attachment style is expressed when we have a negative image about ourselves, but a positive image about everyone else. People with this attachment style believe they can't get close to others and develop intimate relationships because they will be seen as unworthy. They have a strong desire to get close to people and develop rich, happy relationships but think others will find them unworthy of love. They value intimacy so much that they often become completely dependent on their attachment figure. Anxiousness will pass only when they are in direct contact with their attachment figure, a partner.

These people are also often impulsive in action, oversensitive and over emotional, they worry too much and constantly blame themselves for a partner's lack of response.

Dismissive-avoidant attachment style: Expressed when a person has a positive image of himself but negative of others. People with this attachment style are comfortable without depending on anyone; they do not need a close emotional relationship. They are overly independent and self-sufficient. They also don't like others to depend on them. They see dependence as weakness. The desire of complete independence will make these people not need any kind of attachment figure; they will hide their true feelings and consider themselves invulnerable to relationship problems. They will often consider relationships not necessary, and when faced with rejection, they will quickly deal with it by distancing themselves from partners.

Fearful-avoidant attachment style: Comes to expression in people who have an uncertain, confused, and unstable image of themselves and others. It usually develops in those who've had stressful past experiences, such as sexual abuse or some other type of trauma. They feel uncomfortable getting close to others due to fear that the trauma will repeat. They do want and crave emotional relationships, but their own fear stops them from trusting others and open themselves up. They worry they will get hurt no matter what, and they think their attachment figure isn't being honest about their intentions. They often deny their own feelings and are not comfortable expressing affection.

Attachment style matrix:

	Anxious	Avoidant
High self-esteem	Secure	Dismissive avoidant
Low self-esteem	Anxious-preoccupied	Fearful avoidant

Belonging to one attachment style or another doesn't mean you are stuck with it. Romantic relationships are a great opportunity to work on yourself and transition from an insecure to a secure attachment style. But there might be situations in your relationship that will hurt you and change your secure attachment style. You have to be careful and assess your partner well before allowing yourself deeper connections and bonds with that person. This is why people like to postpone marriage until the initial feeling of "being in love" or "honeymoon phase" has passed, so they are sure they truly know the person they will spend the rest of their lives with.

If your partner is overly critical and focuses on your mistakes much more than on your success, he might lead you to insecurity. You might have had a beautiful childhood filled with love and security, but the actions of your partner might disrupt you and lead you into a constant feeling of threat and insecurity. This will cause you to question yourself, searching for your partner's approval in all actions you take, and it can lead to total dependency on your partner. If they decide to leave you, this will only deepen your newfound feeling of unworthiness, and you will have trouble connecting with your next partner or new people. This is just a model situation, showing how even later in life we are not well developed because situations and outside influences can still change us.

This model is applicable in a positive form too. If you leave an abusive relationship with strong feelings of unworthiness, but your next partner is loving, reassuring and acknowledges your successes, you might make a transition from the insecure attachment style to a secure one. Allow yourself to see all the good qualities that your partner sees in you and you will prosper and feel confident.

Understanding the attachment style you belong in will only help you work on yourself and your insecurities. If your partner has insecurity issues, understanding his or her attachment styles might give you insight on how to help them feel safe and secure, and how to behave around them. This doesn't mean you should tiptoe in their presence; just be emotionally available and set the example of a good, well-developed attachment system.

Fear of Abandonment

We talked about the importance of a loving, nurturing caregiver who will make us feel secure and safe. This will make a special bond between a child and caregiver who is child's primal attachment figure. But what happens when we are deprived of that figure? What if we are growing up without parents or with parents who are unable to be there when we need them?

What if the parents divorced during our childhood or were disconnected, abandoned us or, even worse, have died?

When we suddenly lose security and stability, we start to experience fear. As children, we are dependent on others for safety and now they are suddenly gone. Fear that comes to replace safety is a natural defense mechanism; it's a healthy survival response. Many people are able to overcome this fear and continue their lives normally, finding security in new attachment figures. There is still a large percentage of people who will develop a pathological connection to fear and will actively search for similar or identical situations. They will become attracted to people who are rejecting them, are too critical, or who are abusive. Your belief that you are trapped in negative emotions or negative behavioral patterns will keep you away from the happiness you deserve. You will feel unworthy of happiness and love, and you will seek only relationships where you will be denied these feelings. You may not have control of the situation that put you in a position to feel like this, but the control is all yours and you are the only one who can change your core beliefs and shut down the fear of abandonment.

Insecurity will lead you to believe your partner will leave you for someone more worthy. If the basis of this fear lies solely in your past experiences and has nothing to do with your current partner, you know that you must work to conquer this fear. It is really hard to control fear. Fear puts us in survival mode and one could say our judgement is clouded by this. Rationality and logic seem far away and unable to reach when we are in survival mode. Fear makes us act based on our instincts. The first instinct

33

when facing fear of abandonment is to accuse the partner; accuse him of not loving you enough, of cheating on you, of showing more interest in everything else but you, etc. This will create ugly situations of arguments and anxiety, and it will deepen the fear and pain you are already dealing with. This is not a healthy way to deal with insecurity. Your partner is only human, and no human reacts positively when being accused or attacked in any way. He will react in ways that will feed your insecurities unless he is aware of your past experiences. This is why communication, yet again, is the only thing that can make the both of you understanding toward each other. If you are able to communicate well with your partner before a stressful situation occurs, he might be aware of how to behave in a given situation and will help you overcome your fears.

Core Beliefs

Your past experiences, especially those from your childhood, will imprint on you and will create something called *core beliefs*. Core beliefs are schemes that allow us to organize information and new experiences. They are a set framework that allow us to orient into new situations. We use them to make sense of our surroundings.

Our core beliefs help us predict new experiences based upon our past experiences, thus allowing us to deal with new situations better. But if your previous experience wasn't a healthy one, it will create problems and make you feel insecure about present and future situations that are similar to that past experience.

We will use fear of abandonment as one of the unhealthy core belief examples. If you had a strong bond with your caregiver and he abandoned you, you will develop a fear of being abandoned. When you enter a relationship and come to rely on your partner, your fear of abandonment will be triggered. Relying on a partner reminds you of relying on the caregiver who abandoned you. Your brain is trying to help you deal with abandonment that didn't happen and won't happen, but it is doing so based on your previous experience.

As we see in the above example, the present and the future is determined by your experiences from the past. Core beliefs are negative or positive ideas that you form about yourself, about others, and about the information you receive from the outside world. They can be either positive or negative, white or black. There is no middle ground or gray areas. This is a good thing because it is quite easy to realize what are your expectations of someone or some situation. Is it good or bad? Will it end up this way or another? Since there are only two choices, it's fairly easy to make a proper decision. The problem starts when your expectations about your partner are constantly negative. You will jump to conclusions that might not be true and your core beliefs will make you insist on them. If your partner seems distracted, you might start thinking that he will leave you soon but the problem might lie somewhere else, for example, in his workplace.

Another example of a negative core belief is when you constantly think negatively about yourself. You then reflect negative feelings and situations on your partner. This is another form of insecurity. Instead of being insecure in your partner's ability to love you and be with you, you are insecure about your worthiness and whether you deserve your partner's love.

There are five negative core beliefs tightly bound to insecurities, and together they work to ruin a relationship:

1. Abandonment: A core belief based on loss. It can be either the physical loss of a loved one or an emotional loss, when we suddenly stop receiving reassuring emotions from our attachment figures.

2. Mistrust: A core belief that developed in childhood when we experienced abuse, betrayal, humiliation or manipulation. A person with this core belief dives into relationships with the expectation of being hurt, cheated, and lied to.

3. Emotional deprivation: This core belief can develop if needs for emotional support aren't being met. It can be the absence of attention, affection, understanding, and deprivation of protection. A person with this core belief will enter relationships believing he doesn't deserve support and attention, and he will also be emotionally closed.

4. Defectiveness: This belief makes a person think he is unworthy of love. It can be because of some inner flaw one might have, such as questioning his intelligence or some flaw that leads a person to

believe their looks aren't good enough.

5. Failure: People expect failure in everything they do. One will feel inadequate to perform certain tasks, therefore, he won't try because he thinks failure is imminent. Even if they do have a success, they feel guilty as they feel it isn't deserved.

To better understand your insecurities, it's important to be aware of your core beliefs so you can take control of them. Start a journey through your own childhood memories and see if your personal story has anything to do with the challenges you now face in your relationship. Remember, this journey might be very painful; it may be smart to involve your partner, a friend you trust, or a therapist. Memories can trigger some negative feelings such as anxiety, sadness, and shame. Be sure you do not react impulsively in the presence of these feelings as they could become even worse. Don't blame yourself or others for your past experiences, this journey is not about blame. It is about bringing awareness to your beliefs, so you can start the healing process within you. Make peace with your past and move forward into a happier life. Once you understand your core beliefs, you will be able to better assess the situations when they rise up and respond to them accordingly. Your behavior will change and you will stop hurting yourself and your partner with your own insecurities.

Chapter 4: Other Common Fears and Insecurities in a Relationship

In previous chapters we mentioned some fears and insecurities one might have that will negatively influence relationships. We mentioned them as either a source of insecurity or a product of one. But there are many more, and each could influence a person's life in another way. Some will manifest in a relationship, but they can also ruin other aspects of life, such as work, creativity, health, and social life. In this chapter, we will try to number as many as we can. Recognizing some or all of them will help you to understand where they are coming from, how they can influence you, and how you can deal with them.

Lack of Self-Esteem

Lack of self-esteem, or low self-esteem, is the absence of confidence in yourself. People with low self-esteem will often feel bad about themselves and will be in constant fear of being exposed, ridiculed, and judged. They think of themselves as unlovable people and feel social anxiety. They might feel incompetent to perform some easy, everyday tasks. People who lack self-esteem may be hypersensitive. It is very easy to hurt them as they don't take criticism well.

Low self-esteem can also make a person be hypervigilant. They will see disapproval, judgement, and rejection when there is none. They see themselves as always making mistakes doing embarrassing things. They are constantly aware of situations that will put them in a negative light and expose them.

We are all vulnerable to criticism to a certain degree. But we are also able to get back on track and perform better. An insecure person will be in a constant phase of low self-esteem; they do not have coping mechanisms that will lift them up above a problematic situation and will keep dwell on fear of others. This may be because they are overcriticizing themselves. They are their own worst enemies. They are the first to pass negative judgement on their own thoughts and behaviors. They perceive themselves as incapable to do anything right. When we have this negative opinion of ourselves, we expect others to have it about us too. People with low self-esteem will often label themselves awkward, shy or anxious, and they will act that way to conform to the label and convince others. It's difficult to believe that others might see past our flaws and perceive our positive traits. Life of a person with low self-esteem can be very difficult.

How to deal with low self-esteem

There are two things you must master in order to overcome a lack of self-esteem. The first is to stop criticizing yourself and stop listening to inner monologues of self-judgment. The second is to become self-compassionate.

Your inner judgment might sound like this:

"You are ugly."

"You are not funny."

"You are worthless."

"Every time you open your mouth you embarrass yourself."

"Be more like your sister."

"Nobody will ever love you."

This is often the everyday thought pattern of a person with low self-esteem. It is an ugly world. To stop criticizing yourself the next time one of these thoughts comes to mind, try to challenge it. Try writing your negative thoughts in one column and in the next write the positive counterpart of that thought. It's not important at this moment if you believe in that positive counterpart. Every time a negative one comes to your mind, read the positive and trust that in time you will become just that.

Example:

I am ugly	I am pretty
I am not funny	I have an interesting sense of humor
I am stupid	I am intelligent and competent
Be more like your sister	Be your amazing self

The trick here is to defy your own criticism. Challenge it and give yourself options. This way, you will exit the enchanted circle of putting yourself back into negative thoughts that will feed your insecurity and lower your self-esteem.

Self-compassion is nothing more than being your own best friend. How would you treat your friends who are in a difficult situation? You would encourage them and offer support and compassion. All of this you can do for yourself. Self-compassion is not confidence, and it is not the opposite of self-esteem; it's even better. It teaches you kindness and acceptance. Self-compassion does not come naturally, and we have to practice it. It may even feel pretty awkward to think this way about yourself, but it will become easier with time and practice.

This is what you should do to practice your self-compassion:

1. Be aware of your self-judgment. Do not let it consume you; allow it to quickly pass.

2. Take care of yourself when you feel negative emotions (perform breathing exercises, take a relaxing bath, meditate).

3. Remember that everyone has flaws and that's what makes us human. You are not any different. This will help you accept your flaws and not see them as something exclusively negative.

4. Write a letter to yourself from the perspective of a kind friend. Read the letter whenever you battle your inner judgment or whenever you are afraid of other people's judgments.

5. Observe other people's compassion and kindness and learn from them. Observe how your loving friends treat you or their own

loved ones. Parents are amazing supporters, and it might be wise to observe how they treat their children when they are sick, hurt or anxious.

There is one more thing you can do to feel better about yourself. It has less to do with directly building self-esteem, but it will help you learn how to interact with others in a positive way, and you will learn how to be kind and compassionate. It is all about doing something meaningful for others and yourself. Try volunteering at a local pet shelter or hospital. Try being there for elderly people, read to them or have conversation to pass their time. Volunteering has a positive influence on one's self-esteem. The goal here is to do a task that is bigger than yourself and helping others will put you into a mindset to think more about their needs and how to help them, and less about judging your own actions and thoughts.

Inferiority Complex

When a person constantly doubts himself, he feels uncertainty and believes he cannot measure up to set standards, he has an inferiority complex. These standards can be set either by ourselves or by others, usually parents and romantic partners. The inferiority complex is subconscious and it can influence a person in a positive way, making them try hard and achieve spectacular success. But more often it will lead to extreme asocial behavior, anxiety, anger, or even aggressiveness.

The term inferiority complex is developed by psychologist Alfred Adler and it represents an intense feeling of not belonging or feeling of "being less than."

The Adlerian movement in psychology recognizes primary and secondary inferiority feelings, making a distinction in origin of the complex and how it manifests:

1. Primary inferiority feelings come from our own childhood experiences. At some point in our past, we felt extreme helplessness and dependency on our caretaker and instead of receiving support and compassion, we are being compared to our siblings or adults. We later transfer this behavior and compare ourselves to our romantic partner, expecting to achieve the same things as they do. When this doesn't happen and we fail, we don't feel good enough, or inferior in comparison to our loved one.

2. Secondary inferior feelings appear in adulthood. It is the inability to achieve the goals we set. These goals we often set so we can compensate for our childhood feeling of inferiority. Not being able to reach our goals will make us feel depressed. If we observe how it comes easily to our partners to achieve their own goals, it will make us feel less capable than them and put us in an awkward position of inferiority. We will start to observe ourselves as not worthy of our partners.

It is important to be able to recognize the first signs of inferiority complex to understand ourselves and to properly seek help if needed. The signs of inferiority complex are:

1. **Social withdrawal:**

People who battle inferiority complex are often antisocial. They do not enjoy the company of others as they have a constant feeling that they do not belong and that others will realize that and won't accept them. It is also very hard for a person with an inferiority complex to make new friends or maintain old friendships because of the constant feeling of not being good enough, therefore not liked by others.

2. **Fault finding:**

People with inferiority complex will seek to make others feel bad about themselves. This is due to their inability to see positive achievements and enjoy them. They constantly seek inability in others to ease the pain of feeling inadequate and to affirm that others are just like them, and to approve of their feelings of inferiority.

3. **Performance anxiety:**

Fear of failure, being laughed at and being judged is very strong in people with an inferiority complex. They will feel extreme anxiety when asked to perform even the meaningless everyday tasks in front of others. Because they expect failure, they are putting themselves in the mindset that will ensure failure and they believe they cannot perform the task.

4. **Craving for attention:**

Individuals with inferiority complex need constant validation and approval from others to feel happy. They are completely unable to feel positive about themselves, therefore they need an outside source. They will ask for attention and they will be overly dependent on it. They may even pretend to be sick to receive much needed attention so they can feel happiness.

5. Oversensitivity:

Inferiority complex makes people highly sensitive to what others think or say about them. Even if it's a compliment or positive, constructive criticism they are unable to take it well and they might become aggressive. This is because every thought they have about themselves is being confirmed by criticism or judgment, and they react too emotionally.

Complete Dependency on the Partner

People who suffered separation anxiety, a chronic illness or had overprotective parents during childhood may develop dependent personality behaviors. Later in adulthood, this reflects on their relationship as being overly dependent on their partners, even to the point when simple, everyday tasks are impossible to achieve without their partner's approval or involvement.

Feeling the need for your partner too often is not a sign of love, but of fear and insecurity. When your happiness depends solely on your partner, the validation and attention you get from him becomes like an addiction. You are unable to function normally without it, and you start to doubt the world and yourself.

Being completely emotionally dependent on your partner will eventually lead to losing yourself, and you will have a feeling like there is no life outside your relationship. A codependent relationship is nothing more than unhealthy clinginess, which makes you lose your autonomy. It's important to spend your own time with your friends and family. Do not allow your partner to become the only person you interact with.

A codependent person will feel anxiety and stress when thinking about doing something on their own. It is natural to want to spend as much time as possible with our partner, especially in a new relationship, but feeling stressed when your partner is not around is a sign of too much dependency.

Finding happiness solely in your relationship is a symptom of a deeper insecurity. Codependency might come as a symptom of low self-esteem, a need for validation from your partner, or from a fear of abandonment. In any case, being codependent means you need help to search for the insecurity that's causing it. Being able to deal with it will lead to a happier, self-fulfilled life.

Fear of Betrayal

Trust is something we build over time; it is not freely given. It needs to be earned. Many of us have been betrayed in one way or another by parents, friends, teachers, or partners. It is hard to build up trust again, but we do manage. This is because we need to feel trust so we can rely on people around us and feel safe. Without the feeling of safety, we would be lonely and depressed.

People with insecurity may have an irrational fear of building a relationship with their partner because they are unable to give their full trust. This can be due to some past events during childhood when parents broke a promise or due to a previous relationship when an ex cheated on us. It can be anything. Healthy people are able to recover the trust and not live with the fear of betrayal from their new partner, but an insecure person will believe that it is just a matter of time when the new partner will betray or disappoint them. They are afraid that the past harms they endured may reappear, and they will have to relive that traumatic event.

It is not as if they don't want to love and trust again. It is a feeling of inability to heal old wounds. Because of this, they often feel disappointment about themselves, anger, anxiety, sadness, and even shame for being incapable of trust.

People who live in fear of betrayal will never take any risks that might endanger their emotions. They are closed, and they don't like to share their emotions. A partner might see them as distant and cold. They seem introverted and solitary; they don't like to share the events of the day with their partner, fearing their own emotions will be used against them.

As we can see, the fear of betrayal comes from insecurity that is closely related to trust, but not only the trust in their partner, but also themselves. They do not trust their own judgment and intuition, therefore it's easier to live believing you will end up being hurt. Building a relationship with a constant fear of betrayal is an almost impossible task. The fear of being hurt stops a person from putting an effort into a relationship, and the relationship will stagnate. This is why people who are afraid of betrayal are more likely to end the relationship without any explanation given. They are just simply unable to live with that fear anymore, and ending the relationship seems as only possible "getaway."

Escaping this cycle of fear and of betrayal will require some serious work and time. Gaining trust takes time, so is the healing process as a whole. It is important to learn how to properly grieve betrayal to overcome it. Pain won't just go away, we have to learn how to manage it. Before stepping into a new relationship, it is best to make sure we overcome our fears to the healthy degree. Stabilize your emotions and take time to be ready to trust someone again. Most of all, learn how to trust your own judgement and intuition. They are important self-protection mechanisms that will warn you in time and make you able to avoid harmful events.

Although it's hard to start trusting someone, it is extremely beneficial in relationships. The feeling of security will boost your self-confidence and overall happiness; it will allow you to face the challenges of a relationship in a healthy way, and it will take off the stress from uncomfortable situations that arise in relationship.

Jealousy in Relationship

It is a widespread misconception that jealousy is a sign of love. How many times did we hear statements such as "He wouldn't be jealous if he didn't care?" We even see titles like these in magazines and online articles every day. Psychology warns us that jealousy is a natural feeling, and we all experience it from time to time. It is a defensive mechanism that warns us that something might be wrong, and we need to work on our relationship more. But it doesn't necessarily mean we need to blame our partner for infidelity. Jealousy is most often a product of our own insecurity. Our own fear that we will be abandoned, that our partner will find someone more worthy of his/her love, and, yes, it is a sign we need to work, not just on our relationship, but on ourselves. We need to find the root cause of feeling jealousy. There are several traits we all might have that can lead to jealousy:

1. Low self-esteem

2. Unstable emotions, prone to anxiety

3. Possessiveness

4. Unnatural dependence on your partner

5. Feeling of inadequacy; feeling of not being good enough

6. Fear of abandonment

All these traits constitute insecurity in relationships. As you can see none of these traits is about love for a partner; they are representations of one's own insecurities.

Dealing with jealousy the right way will help your relationship and also help you as an individual to deal with insecurities and put you on the right track to lead a normal, healthy life.

How to Deal with your own jealousy

There are actions you can take to prevent jealousy, and the work is solely on you. Let's be honest, in some situations jealousy can be justified. For instance, when your partner previously cheated on you and you chose to stay with him/her, when you don't have the same relationship goals as your partner, when he or she is not ready to commit to one person, or when your partner betrayed your trust in some way. If you do get jealous without a logical reason, as we like to say, "Over stupid things," you are the root problem, and jealousy is from your own insecurity. When this happens and you are aware that it is your insecurity is from you, there are actions you may want to take to prevent emotional outbursts that can ruin your relationship.

1. Don't act on jealousy:

Jealousy is a very strong feeling and there is an urge to react explosively in situations that provoke us. It's really hard not to act on jealousy, and it can take a tremendous amount of strength to avoid it. Never punish yourself for the existence of feelings of jealousy. It is important to learn how to control yourself and not take actions that will create unpleasant situations. Remember that your partner is human, and he might find someone else attractive. This doesn't mean he will engage himself with that other person. There is a reason why he is with you; you are offering him so much more than attraction. Remember he loves you for who you are. If he wanted to date someone else, he would do so, but he is with you. That means he wants to be with you. So, remember, it's okay to feel jealousy; you're human too. But be wise about it and change the way you think. There's no real danger behind your jealousy and there is no need to create situations you will later regret.

2. Be vulnerable:

If your jealousy is stirred yet again, stay calm. The next thing you can do to help your relationship is to open up to your partner and make yourself emotionally available. Remember that this partner was your choice, and you love him with reason. Have faith in him and in yourself. You are able to deal with the unknown situations and you need to be willing to accept them. The risks will happen; your partner does have a life beyond you, and it's not up to you to control his or hers life. You are there not just to receive the support, but also give it.

3. Communicate

Just as you are allowed to feel jealousy, you are allowed to express it. But be smart about it and do it in soft way. There is no reason for compulsive quarrels and panic attacks. You are a mature person and so is your partner. It's only natural that you two are able to communicate in a well-mannered, mature way. You can approach the topic of jealousy in different ways. It's important that your partner receives the information in the most natural way for him. If he is not humorous person, don't try to joke about it. But if he is, this might be the best way to approach it. Laugh about it together and you will feel the jealousy leave. Another approach is to have diplomacy.

Be smart about it and start by saying that you love him and how much he means to you. Tell him that his behavior caused you discomfort, but you are aware he will never cheat on you. You can also choose to be direct, but some people aren't receptive to directness. Asses your partner and use good judgment if this is the best way to approach the topic of jealousy. Some people respond to directness well, but others will feel attacked. If being direct, don't forget to say you trust your partner and put emphasis on your awareness of being unable to control your feelings. Ask them nicely to take into consideration your feelings the next time they find themselves in a situation that may lead to jealousy.

4. Appreciate yourself

Insecure people feel they are not worthy of the love that a partner gives them. They never feel good enough and think their partner will start to search for someone better. If this feeling is bothering you, imagine looking through your partner's eyes. If you do need confirmation and reassurance from him, don't hesitate to ask for it, but be reasonable about it. Don't do it often and approach it smart. You don't need to ask him to constantly repeat that he loves you. Instead, ask for the reasons why he loves you. This will allow you to see yourself through their eyes. Nourish the positive traits your partner loves and learn to appreciate yourself. The next time you feel jealous, remember there are reasons your partner is with you.

5. Take time to heal

If your previous partner cheated on you or hurt you in any way, it's normal to feel insecure and jealous. It's is also important to remind yourself that your new partner is not your ex. Remember that you are in no danger and allow yourself to heal those old wounds. You must understand the root of your insecurities lie in your past, and your past cannot hurt you anymore. Allow your experience to make you stronger and help you to become a better person. Also, it is important to communicate with your new partner and tell them about your past and ways that your ex hurt you. This will give your partner an understanding of your feelings so he can avoid situations that will leave you feeling threatened or jealous.

6. Trust

Trust is a critical ingredient necessary for a happy relationship, and, honestly, you do not have much choice. If you want a happy relationship, you have to build trust between you and your partner. We all sometimes have this unreasonable urge to control our partners life, but when we start acting on it, it becomes a big problem. No one is allowed to control another person, and no one really can. Your partner had a life before you and is having a life with you, but he also has a life parallel with yours and you do not have a control over it. You have to let go of your insecurities and jealousy to live a healthy life, and to be in a healthy relationship. Trust your partner and love him despite your feelings of jealousy.

7. Believe in yourself

Simply put, believe that you are capable of controlling your emotions. You have full control over jealousy, and you cannot allow it to consume you. You are strong and reasonable. You are capable of using logic and not allowing emotions to overtake you. Trust in your capability to love your partner and have confidence that you will be able to deal with all situations.

8. Don't be afraid to seek help

If your feeling of jealousy is too strong and you are losing control over it, don't be afraid to seek outside help. Sometimes your parents might be the ones with words of wisdom, and friends can give you an outside perspective on your relationship. Be careful, and don't let just anyone meddle in your intimate life. Share only what you and your partner feel comfortable sharing. Don't put him in a position to lose your trust. Sometimes it's good to seek couples counseling or individual therapy to help you cope with your extreme feelings of jealousy.

How Insecurity Affects Partners

Feeling insecure will create situations in relationships that are not pleasant. Insecurity doesn't affect just one person, it affects the whole relationship and your partner will feel it too. In the beginning he or she will be supportive, will fulfill all your needs, and maybe even find cute the constant attention an insecure person needs. But, honestly, how many times can one repeat that everything is okay? Constant reassurance will make your partner tired of repeating himself. This will at first lead to small quarrels and in time will lead to big fights that will threaten to destroy your relationship. Insecurity is not attractive and it will, in time, put your partner off. This doesn't mean he doesn't love you enough. Patience is not limitless, and he will become aware he is not in a healthy relationship. Insecure people can even become abusive with constant demands of reassurance.

An Insecure person can display various behaviors that are extremely off putting and will destroy an otherwise happy relationship:

1. The constant need to see your partner, the desperation to talk to him, or just "hold on" to him can be extremely tiresome for both sides. Your partner will have to commit extra time to devote to you, and his other aspects of life may suffer. This means that he will have to cut the time he planned for work, family, friends and invest it in your relationship. This is not healthy. Everyone needs to have time for their own interests and obligations and your partner will become aware that the relationship he has with you is not healthy.

2. Accusations of your partner not loving you enough, cheating on you, or finding others more interesting to be around than you. Here we have to make a difference between intuition and insecurity. Intuition may be a product of hidden facts and clues we see around us of our partner being unfaithful. Intuition is that gut feeling that something is wrong and is based on existing problem such as: your partner suddenly changed his behavior or he is spending time with an unknown person. But when it comes to insecurity, the reasoning is illogical, and there is no gut feeling. There is just constant, mind-numbing fear that your partner is unfaithful. This fear doesn't have a basis in your relationship and is often not even connected to your partner. You may be suffering from some past experience with adultery, and you are reflecting it

on your partner. He will have to prove over and over again that he is faithful and that you are the only one. In time, this becomes frustrating and will develop anxiety in your partner. Again, he is aware of the unhealthy nature of your relationship.

3. You constantly need to check up on your partner. You are looking through his phone, his email, and work schedules. You are not only searching for proof that you are right, you're feeding your fears and insecurities.

Chapter 5: Behavioral Reactions and Their Triggers

The amygdala is the part of our brain that plays an important role in how we respond to fear. It also guides our emotions, determines how we react to certain situations and to other people. It plays a part in shaping our social lives as well as relationships. When we feel threatened, it is first to react. It receives the threat as an impulse before it reaches our neocortex, the part of the brain that will rationalize our fears, and this is why we have impulsive reactions, almost instinctive, and we're unable to control them.

This phenomenon is also called the amygdala hijack. When we experience a threat that results in powerful emotions, they overwhelm us, and we can't think rationally, which can lead to a series of behaviors that are hurtful to ourselves. These behaviors might relieve immediate pain, but in the long term they are actually hurting your relationship.

There are three main behavioral reactions to our insecurities manifested as fear, and can be explained as fight, flight or freeze responses.

The fight behavioral reaction to insecurities: means that we are impulsively accusing, blaming, and criticizing our partner when we find ourselves in situations that trigger our insecurity. To achieve our goal, we try to control our partner. We also try to achieve a great accomplishment to get the attention of our partner. We can even surprise ourselves with our ability to manipulate and exploit our partner (this includes seduction and lying to achieve our goal). Rebellion is another behavioral reaction to insecurity, together with passive-aggressiveness. We may seem compliant and wanting to please but pretend we are unable to do so.

The freeze behavioral reaction to insecurity: includes compliance and complete dependence. We rely too much on our partner, allowing him to make all decisions even if they are not good for us. We will behave passively and avoid conflict as much as possible.

The flight behavioral reaction to insecurity: is defined by total isolation, autonomy, and independence. We search for distraction in other activities that don't include our partner or have nothing to do with our relationship. People who often express this type of behavior, when confronted with their insecurities, may seek excitement in drugs, alcohol, food or other addictive, self-soothing stimuli. The flight behavioral reaction makes people try to escape through fantasy, denial, or emotional withdrawal.

You may recognize one or more behavioral reactions in yourself. They are tightly close to the core beliefs we possess during our childhood experiences. Being aware to what group of core beliefs and behavioral reactions you belong is a great step in fighting them. When a situation that triggers your fear presents itself, you will be aware that your reactions are not rational but rather impulsive and instinctive. This will give you power to overcome and control them, and you will find more effective ways of dealing with insecurity.

There are common behaviors of others, especially your partner, that will trigger your core belief and your insecurity, and make you react with fight, flight or freeze response.

The **abandonment core belief** is one of the easiest one to trigger because it has roots in our survival instinct. These are some of the behaviors your partner might show that will trigger your abandonment insecurity:

1. Sudden change in behavior. For example, your partner sends you text messages every night before going to bed. One night you don't receive a message, and immediately your thought process is changed to "What if he leaves me?"

2. Your partner has a relationship that might threaten your own. It can be a friendship with the opposite sex. Your own insecurity will interpret your partner's friendship as a sign that he likes her and that he will soon leave you for her.

3. Your partner might show behavior that seems like rejection. For example, during a call he is distracted by work. Your insecurity will translate this as he is not interested in you.

4. Longer periods of separation. Your partner has to go on a business trip. Your insecurity makes you believe that it's a lie and you fear he is abandoning you.

5. An argument over the smallest thing may trigger your abandonment anxiety and make you think he is ready to leave.

When abandonment insecurities are triggered, a person might react by becoming clingy. They may start arguments just to test their relationship and a loved one. They also may close up and not show emotion so when abandonment happens, they don't get hurt.

Abuse and mistrust core belief may be triggered by:

1. You partner feels anger, your insecurity will make you believe he intended to hurt you.
2. Your partner is criticizing you. An insecure person sees it as a personal threat rather than a constructive, well-meant objection.
3. When your partner is interested in getting to know you better, you might feel his intentions are to gather information to be able to manipulate or hurt you directly.
4. Your partner's desire for intimacy may come as an attempt of abuse to those who suffered any type of abuse in the past.

When the abuse and mistrust core beliefs are triggered, a person might constantly be looking for any sign of betrayal or abuse. They may be suspicious of a partner's motives of kindness and love. People with these insecurities will never show how vulnerable they are and will allow mistreatment because they believe they deserve it.

The **emotional deprivation core belief** is triggered when your partner:

1. Lacks understanding or interest in you.

2. Does not express his emotions in a way you desire.

3. Doesn't ask what your needs are.

4. Doesn't initiate deeper emotional connection with you.

When emotional deprivation is triggered you can become far more demanding as a person. You become attracted to people who are not showing their emotions, you shut yourself off emotionally and never show your weaknesses. You may also come to resent your partner for not giving you the love and understanding that you crave for.

Behaviors your partner might express that will trigger **defectiveness core belief**:

1. Disappointment in you. This might not be real, but your insecurities make you believe your partner is somehow disappointed with you.

2. The same with disapproval. It might not exist, but you firmly believe your partner is not approving your actions.

3. Absent reassurance. Insecurities make us crave constant reassurance. Your partner might not indulge you.

When defectiveness is triggered by your partner, you might find yourself criticizing other people but you won't accept any criticism of yourself, hiding your thoughts and actions. You might demand reassurance by comparing yourself to others.

The **failure core belief** is triggered when:

1. Your partner compares you to others, even with the best of intentions. You see it as a personal failure due to your insecurity.

2. Any kind of criticism, constructive or destructive, will make us reassure ourselves that we are failures.

3. Even if other people show a desire to get to know you, you might see it as your personal failure to be invisible for others.

4. The success of your partner can make you feel unworthy of him. You might feel he deserves someone better.

When failure insecurities are triggered, you will try to avoid discussions and arguments. You allow others to minimize your accomplishments, talents, and potentials. You are also do it to yourself. You constantly compare yourself to others and think you will never be as good as they are.

Make sure you recognize your partner's behavior that triggers your core beliefs. Communicate with him and explain how he can help you overcome your insecurities.

Chapter 6: Love Insecurity in Digital Age

We live in the so called digital age, where the internet is available to almost everyone and we can't really imagine our lives without it anymore. Smartphones are the norm and all the social media applications that come with it. Facebook, Twitter, Instagram, and other social networks are designed to make it easier to keep in touch, but they also open up a whole new world of possibilities that may threaten existing relationships.

Psychology today recognizes two types of Digital Romantic Insecurities, and, yes, this is the officially recognized name for a special kind of insecurity. First is when a person's insecurity is fed by a partner's use of social networks and the internet in general. A person might feel threatened by the possibility of a partner meeting someone else online. The other one concerns couples and their insecurities when they use social networks to post about their relationship in search of validation from the outside.

Personal Insecurity in the Digital Age

Social networks, such as Facebook, Instagram and Twitter, may increase one's feelings of insecurity. As we mentioned before, insecurity can be rooted in childhood experiences or previous relationships. But social networks will deepen insecurities and enhance emotional pain for the one affected.

Social media is tightly bound to feelings of jealousy, which is a symptom of insecurity. It is a fertile ground for building distrust in relationships and for increasing one's fear of betrayal.

The age of social media is putting new pressure on people. So much depends on likes, tweets, and followers. We seek validation from others, and today a "like" is considered validation and we feel we have achieved something. An insecure person may see a mere like as a sign of flirting, and it will create a number of possibilities as to what it really means. If your partner receives one, or a message from an unknown person of the opposite sex, an insecure person will light up with red flags, feeling threatened.

Social media is also known for reconnecting with ex partners. This will negatively influence your current insecure partner. There will be myriad questions going through his mind: "Does he still love his ex?" "Are they seeing each other again?" "Was she better than me?" "Will he leave me for her?" These insecurities we might see as positive traits as they must really care for us if they feel threatened by an ex. We find it cute and we take it as a sign of true love. But what happens when our insecure partner has an irrational fear of abandonment stirred up by these questions? What if your partner starts acting on his or her insecurities? Emotional outbursts are not easy to deal with, and if your loved one is pressured by impulsive panic arising from fear of abandonment, anxieties will deepen and quarrels will rise. They could even act aggressive and outright attack you.

Is there a solution that will help to avoid insecurity-triggered emotional outbursts? You may be attracted to the idea of closing up, hiding your social network from your partner, or hiding away when chatting with other people. Keep in mind that if your insecure partner feels threatened once, he will convince himself that he is not good enough and will actively search for evidence to reassure his feeling of inadequacy. He will accuse you of being the one who is at fault and you will create an even bigger mess. So, what can you do to keep tension low with insecure partner and keep using social media? The answer is communication. Be open emotionally, be supportive, and show how much you care and love your partner. When people feel loved, there is no reason to search for evidence of infidelity. This is not a "How to avoid your partner finding out," this is "How to show you truly care and want to help your insecure partner." Be open about your social network with your partner and even involve him or her to show that there is nothing to be worried about.

Nowadays, most people treat social media as extensions of themselves. Their insecurities make them seek attention and validations from their peers on social networks. They also demand their partner's constant interaction with what they post online. If he doesn't immediately like, comment or respond to their post, they see it as a sign that he stopped caring and loving them. Many people admit feeling this way about social media and their romantic relationships. Today, the success of one's relationship is measured by the interaction of your loved one with your personal online content.

Couple's Insecurity in Digital Age

We all know a couple or have been in a relationship with someone who constantly posts about their love life, relationships, and their partners. They love reminding their followers how in love they are and how great their relationship is. They will post pictures of their anniversary, vacations, and they will update their status with cheesy love messages directed to their partner or will update the public with what the two of them have been doing. They have a need to prove how their relationship is happy while behind the screen it's a completely different story.

Just like with personal insecurities, couples seek validation from the public, reassurance that what they are doing is good. Social scientists came up with a term "relationship visibility" to address the need to make our relationships public. Studies show that people with the need for high relationship visibility are most often the couples with deep insecurities about their relationship. It is also believed that attachment styles (the way we emotionally bond to others) directly influences our desire to post about our relationships.

People with a dismissive-avoidant and a fearful-avoidant attachment style will show less desire to expose their relationships on social media. An anxious attachment style person will show increased need for relationship visibility because of their need for reassurance, not only from their partner as attachment figure but from the public as well. Researchers found no correlation between secure attachment style and the desire for relationship visibility.

People with anxious attachment style show the need to document events that reassure their insecurities about their relationship. For example, a romantic dinner date. A secure attachment style person will be able to completely enjoy the date. An anxious type will have to snapchat and post about it as it happens while an avoidant attachment style person will feel content with a quiet date. If the anxious type is in a relationship with an avoidant type, their anxiousness will trigger with their partner's lack of closeness and reassurance. They will seek much needed reassurance elsewhere, often on social media where one like is enough to make them feel good about the relationship. They seek the attention they are unable to get from their partner and often post about their relationship to get attention.

Remember, each couple has a unique story and maybe they just want to highlight joyful events by sharing them on social media, and they don't have insecurities. But when it comes to oversharing to the point of being annoying, it probably means that couple is struggling with their relationship and have a strong need to show the perfect picture even though it is not realistic. This is one way of how they cope with their problems. Don't be too quick to judge them. Soon enough, if they are wise about it, they will overcome their problems one way or another.

Chapter 7: Inner Critical Voice

The inner critical voice comes from our defense system that we developed as children. No matter how loving and nurturing our parents were, there is no such thing as perfect parenting. They were not capable of seeing and responding to all the needs we might have had as children, and this is completely normal. Every child experiences some kind of frustration, anxiety or pain, and develops his own defensive mechanisms that will make sure a similar situation, when and if it arises, doesn't hurt us again. These defensive systems stay in place throughout our childhood, adolescence and adulthood, even though we are now perfectly capable of dealing with stressful situations in a more natural and mature way because we don't depend on others for survival.

The critical inner voice is the internal dialogue we have with ourselves that supports our defensive system. It is the encouragement we need to not get too close to someone, not to show our emotions and not to be vulnerable when in the presence of others, all in anticipation of being hurt. The inner critical voice is encouraging our self-hate and makes us cynical toward the other. The language of our inner critical voice is often filled with irony.

A critical inner voice should not be mixed up with hallucinations. It is more of a negative thought process that happens. It often degrades our accomplishments and reminds us that we are unworthy of love. We accept our inner voice as the truth, after all, who knows us better than ourselves? The problem is, we often have a wrong picture of ourselves because of our critical inner voice. It is a way of destructive negative thinking that is capable of undermining and even destroying a relationship.

How an Inner Critical Voice Attacks Your Relationship

One of the ways your inner voice may attack your relationship is by first attacking you. You will start by feeling negative, thinking negative and then acting on those negative feelings and thoughts. Your responses will be aggressive and destructive for the relationship. The inner critical voice will make you believe you are not worthy of your partner's love. It will nag about all your flaws, reinforcing self-hatred. In time, this will create a distance between you and your partner. You will withdraw into yourself and stop being emotionally available. This is a fine recipe for destroying a romantic relationship.

The second way the inner voice attacks a relationship is by bombarding you with negative thoughts about your partner. That might be shown as negative thoughts about how they talk, walk, look, or their habits and personality. The inner voice in your head will exaggerate the flaws of your partner and it will sabotage their successes. It is even possible, in time, to feel open hatred for your partner and this will definitely destroy the relationship.

No matter what way your inner critical voice is destroying your relationship, the basis underlying it is a lie. Our inner voices are nothing more than false perspectives we have of ourselves and our partner. We lie to ourselves because these lies will reaffirm the insecurities we have and

69

make a good excuse and justification as to why we feel insecure in the first place. There are two reasons why we lie to ourselves when it comes to our relationships. One is that we don't want to face reality and the other is we genuinely do not recognize the reality:

1. When we don't want to see reality, we basically refuse to believe in it. For example, our relationship is in turmoil but we are telling ourselves all the little lies to ignore the turmoil itself and we'd rather focus on how we are unworthy of anything better and how we deserve the unhealthy, bad relationship. We convince ourselves that we are a failure, self-hatred consumes us, and we cannot possibly see how our partner could ever love us.

2. We cannot see the reality, we exaggerate the failures and bad personality traits. We convince ourselves with lies that will reinforce the suspicions we might have about our relationship, even if it's a happy one.

How to Fight Your Inner Critical Voice

The inner critical voice is a thought process, and once we are aware of this, it will become easy to give your thoughts a real voice. If you are feeling overwhelmed by negative thoughts, say them out loud. Once you hear them, it will be as if they took a physical form, as they are now exposed and you will be able to confront and fight them.

One of the methods how to fight these thoughts is to put them in second person. The next time your inner voice is attacking you, write down your thoughts and say them out loud, but instead of using "I" try to write them down with "You." Transform "I am unworthy of happiness" into "You are unworthy of happiness." Say out loud, "I am worthy of happiness." Make a plan for next time you have your inner voice attacking you or your relationship. Don't ignore it, rather communicate about it with your partner and be constructive. Include humor in your discussion and laugh together. Instead of being annoyed with your partner's behavior, for example, make a joke of it in a non-hurtful way and show your partner how much you care and love him. Instead of reacting with aggression and destructiveness when your inner voice tries to reinforce your securities, try not acting at all, or doing the complete opposite. It is not simple to counter our defensive mechanisms because they have been with us since childhood and we are not fully conscious of them, but with practice and time it will become easier to counter them, even to the point where we won't have negative thoughts anymore. When this happens, you will be able to enjoy your relationship and its full potential; you will be happy with intimacy and love that you fought for.

Chapter 8: How to Overcome Insecurity in a Relationship

Insecurities come from the past. Each time your insecurity is triggered, you are reliving past events that are holding you back. It's time to move forward and make peace with the past in order to live a happy, fulfilled life with your loved one. The path to achieve a healthy relationship is not an easy one, and it will take time, effort and persistence. In previous chapters, we explained how to recognize your insecurities, what are they and where are they coming from. Understanding all the aspects about your insecurity is an important part of moving forward. Without understanding, you wouldn't be able to make the first steps and invest effort in getting better. Bringing your insecurities to your awareness is already doing wonders, if nothing else, then in motivating you to fight them. Insecurities come as subconscious fears, parts of our defensive mechanisms, tricks and traps of our mind that are holding us back. It is hard to be actively aware, especially in stressful situations and in those first moments when insecurity is triggered. But now you can be aware that it is your inner critical voice speaking; it is not the real you. It's a distorted perception of yourself that is playing with your emotions, using your insecurities to deepen the fear and defend you from being hurt. These defensive mechanisms were useful when we were infants and children. They got stuck with us in adulthood, but now they are bringing more harm than help, and it's time to overcome them.

With the understanding that the problem of your relationship lies in your own insecurities, you should now be aware that not just your thought pattern, but your behavior needs to change too. Your reactions to triggering situations are as harmful as your insecurity, which is undermining you to be happy in a loving, long lasting relationship. But before you try to make any change, what you need is motivation. As mentioned earlier, core beliefs cannot be changed. They have been with us through most of our lives and they are here to stay. The pain that comes with them is something we are often unable to overcome, it's a building block part of your personality. We should not focus on eliminating these beliefs altogether or the pain that comes with them. Instead we should learn how to properly and in a healthy way respond to them when they are triggered.

Acceptance and Commitment therapy (ACT) is making a difference between types of pain we feel when our core beliefs are triggered. First, we recognize *primary pain* and it is a pain that is unavoidable; the pain we feel we can't control and is a part of us. *Secondary pain* is the type of pain we create when trying to avoid and control the primary one. Secondary pain influences the behaviors that are ruining our relationship, and this is the pain that we can control and overcome. You need to learn how to control the things that you have control over, and how to accept the things you can't control. To change one's behavior is a difficult task, but it can be done. All you need are valid reasons that will compel you to push forward.

Learn to Accept

What you've been doing wrong thus far is that you put your effort into controlling your core belief. While doing so, you created new pains that pushed you in behaviors that are harming your relationship. You might have isolated yourself, felt uncontrollable anger, or tried to control others. Your efforts to control the uncontrollable pain were hurting you more and more. It's time to consider changing your tactics. Instead of fighting, it is much healthier to allow yourself to feel all the negative emotions that come when your core belief is triggered. It is time to stop fighting and accept defeat in order to be able to transform. It is hard to accept the defeat, and even harder to understand that you need to feel the pain. But if you do this, you will also feel relieved because you won't have to put all the emotional effort needed when battling an enemy you can't defeat. All the useless struggles you went through trying to control your core belief will go away. The pain will remain, but now that you don't have to fight it, you can listen to it and you might learn something from it.

It might be hard to come to peace with the amount of change you have to go through; the amount of control you need to be able to accept the pain that is a part of you. It might be helpful to think of your painful experience as temporary because it is just that. Think that the situation will go away, but the consequences of your struggles to fight the pain will stay and hurt you even more and create problems in your relationship. When experience that triggers our insecurity is observed as just temporary, it becomes easier to let it go and not react to the experience. We will feel pain, but not reacting to it will give us the calm and objectiveness to repair the damage in our relationship. Put a metaphor in the situation that triggers your core beliefs. It's a storm, the emotions are pretty violent and it puts us in a turmoil, but all storms pass and so will this one. After the storm, sunshine and calm will allow us to repair what's broken and clean the mess that the situation-storm left behind. Do you think you are capable of just letting the storm die out on its own? Negative thoughts we have will always reappear. We can fight them and drive them away for some time, but they will always come back. So, what's the point in being persistent with a strategy that obviously doesn't work? Instead of fighting or avoiding your negative thoughts, try making them helpful. Understand them and accept that they will bring uncontrollable pain, but now you have the strength to experience it and be wiser about it. You are now aware that once the pain goes away, you will be left with much more strength to deal with relationship problems in a much healthier way.

There is a meditation exercise you can do to help you accept the pain caused by your core beliefs:

Sit or lie down comfortably in a place that is very relaxing and where you won't be disturbed by others. Close your eyes and imagine you are a river, water passing by. When thoughts and emotions emerge, imagine them as twigs and leaves carried by the river. Let them pass your vision. You are aware of them for what they are, you are visualizing their temporality as water (you) is carrying them, letting them pass. Even those thoughts and emotions that aren't negative, let them pass. The point of this exercise is to learn how to recognize them for what they are and let go. If you start obsessing over one thought, or one emotion, remember that you are a mighty river and you have the ability to let them go downstream.

Now that you have learned how to recognize and accept your instabilities, you are able to do even more to get rid of them. If not completely, as we learned some of them are imprinted on us as core beliefs, then you will learn how to manage them so they don't hurt your relationship.

Live by Your Values

As we all have imprinted core beliefs, insecurities, we also have imprinted values, characteristics we found useful and that make us happy. These are imprinted on us by our parents, society, and the culture we live in. They are based on morals, personal, and by the society where we grew up. Values vary in different parts of the world, and they can seem pretty personal. It is important to recognize the values you have so you can consciously decide to live by them. Here is a short list of values: Duty, fun, commitment, confidence, affection, clarity, enthusiasm, honor, courage, family, creativity, imagination, freedom, pleasure, loyalty, teamwork, truth, virtue, openness, security, sexuality, wisdom, peace.

These are only some of the possibilities of values. Concentrate and make a list of your values, things that you appreciate the most in others and in yourself.

When our insecurities are triggered by a situation we have no control over, we might behave opposite of our values; we might even surprise ourselves with our behavior and think "This is not me, this is not how I normally behave." That is true. If you don't want that behavior to be part of you, all you need to do is get rid of it. We can't control situations that will trigger us, life is such and they will happen whether we want them. But what we can control is our reaction to them and how we behave. This will stop us from hurting ourselves even more and stop us from hurting our loved ones.

So go ahead and write down your values, be aware of the person you want to become and make a commitment to become that person. Make a promise to yourself that your behavior will reflect your values rather than your

Insecurities.

Next to your value, write down the way how you plan to practice that value:

Openness	Reveal a story from your past to your partner that he or she never heard before
Imagination	Surprise your partner with imaginative and creative dates.
Involvement	Show your partner how much you care by getting involved in his hobbies, family, or anything that he finds important.

Once you manage to replace your negative reactions and behaviors, your relationship will improve significantly, but do not expect it to eliminate all the pain. Remember that pain is coming from core belief that is imprinted in us and as such we don't have control of it. With exercise and patience, you will come to accept it and manage it in a way that is healthy for both you and your relationship.

Negative Thoughts, How They Influence Us and How to Overcome Them

Negative thoughts come from our core beliefs and as such they will never go away. There are people who always seem positive, and it is true they might be more positive than others, but that is due to their own system of core beliefs. There is no such person who doesn't have negative thoughts. We all are victims of our insecurities. They are either better in managing their responses to negative thoughts or their core beliefs are completely different. They might be the lucky ones who grew up in a safe, loving environment but if you ask them they, too, have insecurities and negative thoughts to some degree.

Negative thoughts are cognitive barriers that your relationships are dealing with. When you make progress and turn from insecurities-driven negative behaviors to those driven by your values, you will still find yourself dealing with negative thoughts. If you want to learn how to manage them in a way that won't hurt your relationship, you will have to understand what they are and how they work.

Negative thoughts may come as:

1. Predictions you make based on your core beliefs and past experiences. These may include rejection, abuse, failure, or

abandonment. Predictions are not to be seen as premonitions; they are more expectations. We are so convinced that they are going to happen no matter what and our behavior is leading us into more situations that can cause these expectations to actually happen. This is why we call them predictions.

2. Memories of past situations, losses, and failures. We are prone to remember situations that hurt us much more than the ones that are happy. This is due to our defense mechanisms being at work. We have to remember hurtful situations and experiences to avoid them in future.

3. Negative judgments, that we have about us or the others. Negative judgment comes from insecurities, and it also reflects on others. In them, we see our own insecurities and we easily pass the judgment as a coping mechanism.

As you accepted your core beliefs as something that is constant, and you have no influence over, so should you do with negative thoughts. They come from core beliefs, and we cannot stop them. They will constantly pop up in our minds whether we try to stop them or we don't. The fight you would put in trying to think only positive is futile, there is no amount of strength that will help you achieve this. You may succeed in pushing away negative thoughts temporarily, but they will always come back. You need to accept that negative thoughts happen to everyone and are not controllable. Again, what is controllable is your reaction to them.

At all costs avoid coping behaviors such as drug use, alcohol, gambling, risky sex… These behaviors will numb you so you don't feel emotions that accompany negative thoughts, but you will never get rid of them. This behavior will only create more negative thoughts about yourself and it will spin you in enchanted circle of bad coping mechanisms.

There is a tactic how to properly manage your negative thoughts and it consists of observing, labeling, and letting them go.

Observe your Thoughts

The key to successful observation of your thoughts is objectiveness. It is not easy to be objective when it comes to something as personal as our own thoughts, but it can be learned. Put yourself in a third-person position and use ration and logic to actively engage your thoughts. See how they come to understand them. There is no need to act on them. The next time a negative thought comes to your mind, don't pass the judgment. Instead, take time to ask yourself why did you just think of this? What situation caused your negative thoughts? Where did it come from? Then think if there is a better way to have more positive view on the given situation. Don't be afraid to ask yourself "what if" questions but do it only from objective and rational third-person view.

Label your Thoughts

When you acknowledge your thoughts and when you are able to accept them without judgment, you will take away their power. Putting yourself in the third person will give you the necessary objectivity to observe thoughts, but you will also be able to label them for what they are. Give them names and think of them as what they are: "My abandonment thought" or "Mistrust and abuse thought." Choose a label that works for you and categorize your thoughts. It can even be a thought associated with someone who reminds you of a said thought. For example: when you think "What did I do to deserve my partner?" it might remind you of your experience with your mother. During your schooling she may have been less supportive and frequently asked "What did you do to deserve that grade?" or "What did you do to deserve the main role in the school play?" You can simply label these as "Mom thoughts" if it will make it easier for you to categorize them.

You do not need to write them down, simply practice this in your mind with active thinking. If you do feel the need to write down your thoughts and label them, please feel free to do so. Creating your own ways of dealing with problems is amazing motivation and the path to success.

Let Go of your Thoughts

Remember the meditation exercise we did for letting go of your emotions? We can do the same exercise for thoughts. Instead of emotions, visualize your thoughts passing by, see them as objects you are willing to give up on. Now that you labeled your thoughts, it is easier to visualize them and make them pass by without interacting and reacting to them. Imagine you are driving a car and your thoughts are signs next to the road. Use the labels you gave to your thoughts. Imagine a sign saying, "Mom thoughts" or "Abandonment thoughts." Observe them, acknowledge them and drive past them, letting them go.

Practice observing, labeling, and letting go of your thoughts daily. Practice putting yourself in objective position of a third person to make it easier. Do so with positive thoughts, too, for the sake of practice. In certain situations, it may come as a helpful thing to do with positive thoughts. For example, if you need to hide the excitement so you don't give up on a surprise you are planning for your partner.

Manage Your Emotions

When our insecurities are triggered, what we feel is emotional pain. This emotional pain is responsible for our actions. We react to it, and it makes us behave in unhelpful ways that will only add up to already existing emotional pain. No matter how hard you try, you can't get rid of your negative emotions and thoughts. They always keep reemerging. Just like with behavior and thoughts, you need to learn how to properly manage your emotions. You need to learn how to accept them for what they are even though they are the main reason why you feel the pain.

When your emotions manifest due to your insecurities, you feel pain and you start remembering the situation that caused the insecurity. You start reliving the past, either through your memories or just by feeling the same as you did back then. This will make you blind to the fact that you are in the present and in a different situation. Your behavior will reflect your insecurities, and they will be unhelpful and harm you even more.

Learn to Tolerate your Emotions

There are three main reasons why your emotions keep reappearing:

1. Rumination: when you keep thinking about your past painful experience that caused your insecurity. You won't let go of it and you keep returning to it over and over again.

2. Avoidance: When you don't face your emotions, you keep putting them off. You do not allow yourself to experience your emotions and you can't accept them.

3. Behavior: If your emotions cause you to behave in harmful ways, your emotions will keep coming back even stronger or they will now be caused by your behavior that is endangering your relationship.

What you need to do when your emotions appear is choose the reaction that will not keep hurting you; it won't make you or your partner feel bad, and it won't damage your current relationship. Let's observe what happens with emotions when our insecurity is triggered: once the situation presents itself and you feel at your worst, your emotions are very painful, overwhelming, and you can't bear to feel that way. It is quite normal to want to get rid of them as soon as possible so why should you endure the pain? You start behaving in unnatural ways, ways that are against your own core values. This is why you feel even worse after you let your emotions cause unhelpful behavior. Sometimes these behaviors will make you feel better in the short term, but in the long term, emotions will be back and will strike you even harder.

Emotions are unavoidable, and there is nothing you can do to not feel. What you can control in this situation is a response to your negative emotions. Don't allow them to control your behavior. You are the only one who should have the full control. Accept the responsibility of the way you feel, and don't give in. Adopt behaviors that are healthy and that won't have suffering as a consequence. This is exactly the part you can avoid; the suffering. It is pretty simple. Due to your own insecurity you might want to withdraw socially and disconnect from others completely. As a consequence, this will mean you will miss the opportunity of having good experiences. In time, you will lose your friends, and you will feel lonely and depressed. This is when suffering becomes intolerable. What you need to do is fight your urge to withdraw and close up. You need to allow yourself to feel the emotion but not to give in to it. It has no control over it. You are the one who will decide how to behave in situations that trigger your insecurity. Instead of missing out on friends and good experiences, it's better to join them and cope with your insecurity surrounded with friends who will offer you support. You will not suffer this way.

Distract Yourself from Negative Emotions

If you are afraid that negative emotions are going to overwhelm you and you won't be able to tolerate them, or take control of your behaviors, there is an option of distracting yourself. Be sure to use only healthy distraction activities; this means engage yourself in any helpful and healthy activity that will divert you from the negative emotions you are feeling.

Distracting yourself from emotions will create a window of time that will allow emotions to decrease, and there will be no reason to react on them anymore. The behavior you would execute to feel better will no longer be needed. With your emotions still present, but with lower intensity, you will be cold headed enough to make smart decisions, even observe them objectively, and make proper choices on how to react.

When you distract yourself from negative and hurtful emotions, it doesn't mean you are trying to ignore or forget about them. It is about giving yourself time to clear your head so you can approach the insecurity that caused emotions in the first place with rationality and logic. There are plenty of activities you can partake to distract yourself from strong, negative emotions:

Exercising: Even old Latins had an expression: "Mens sana in corpore sano," which translates to "A healthy mind in a healthy body." They were aware that physical health influences our mental health. This is because exercising releases endorphins, natural pain relievers, and antidepressants. It will make you feel better in general. Endorphin also lowers the levels of cortisol, which is a hormone related to stress. We do not need to mention the health benefits of exercising. It influences your whole body in a positive way. It will help you to lose weight, it will improve oxygen flow and help with elevated blood pressure. Be sure that you choose an exercise that is to your liking. We are not all capable of doing extreme sports no matter how much we want. Start with some light exercises. Even dancing can be a good exercise that will distract you from your emotions.

Hobbies: Another activity that will distract you is engaging in hobbies. It can be anything you want and find interesting. Identify activities you find interesting to and don't wait. Start doing it now. We are often lazy about our hobbies, thinking there is never enough time and there are always more important things to do. Stop thinking like that; hobbies are great way to entertain yourself and stay distracted when needed. It can be anything you find interesting: photography, learning how to play an instrument, cooking, knitting. The possibilities are endless.

Volunteering: Earlier in this book we learned that volunteering is about having a purpose or a task that goes beyond you and your own needs. Helping others puts focus on a good cause that will distract you from what you feel. It also feels rewarding to help someone else. If you want, you can join big organizations that will help you decide how best to spend your time volunteering with the programs they offer or you could do simple stuff such as helping your elderly neighbor shop or walk his dog on a daily basis. It doesn't have to be anything grand. The main thing is to move the focus from yourself to someone else. It will make you feel good about yourself in the most unselfish way.

Tasks: Another great way to distract yourself is to finally do the tasks you were putting off. Especially if you feel stressed under the pressure of emotions. Begin a project you meant to finish but never had the time. Clean the house, build shelves, organize your books, paint your home, do regular house chores. It will also give you needed exercise, and physical work will count. It will release endorphins that will combat your stress and help you feel better about yourself.

Remember, your insecurities in relationships are only yours but your efforts to overcome them are nothing to be selfish about. Whatever way to distract yourself from your emotions that you choose, try to include your partner. Try jogging together or engaging in hobbies you both have an interest in. It will not only help you fight your insecurities, but it can be rewarding for the relationship. Your partner might have insecurities of his own or stresses that you are not even aware of, but they are influencing your relationship. In choosing to share activities, you will both work on your own problems and it will be good for strengthening your relationship.

Change Your Behavior

We discussed how it is impossible to change your core beliefs. You can't change your emotions that are product of your insecurities, but you can change the way you behave to answer those emotions and core beliefs. There are two things you need to do so you can manage to change your behavior successfully: be aware of your current behavior and how it influences your relationship and do the opposite.

Become Aware of your Behavior

Our behaviors that come from insecurities are nothing more than patterns that we must break in order to change the influence of insecurity on our relationship. If you look back on your past behaviors, you will get the best possible chance to change them in future. Don't be ashamed of your past behaviors, and don't think of them as something bad. They were unhelpful, for sure, and that is the only term we need to be aware of. Now we want to change our behaviors to helpful.

Think back to what situations trigger your insecurities. Do you have a response to those situations that repeat themselves? Maybe it is a combination of responses. If you have abandonment insecurities, are you prone to withdraw from your partner but suddenly become clingy and dependent? Do you notice such pattern in your behavior? Feel free to write down your insecurities, what triggers them and how you behave in response to them. Notice the pattern and become aware of it. This will help you see that your previous behavior was harming your relationship, and that it's time to change it. Don't judge your past behaviors, true they might not be pleasant, but behaviors are coping mechanisms meant to deal with emotional pain. They didn't work, but they were the only mechanisms you had. Now you will learn new ones, the helpful ones, and you will see your relationship become more enjoyable for both you and your partner.

To better understand your past behaviors, try to remember how your partner responded to them. Think how your partner behaved immediately after your insecurity triggered and what his long-term response was. Did he get angry? Was he sad? Did he stop calling you? The insecurities are making you behave negatively, and your partner has no other choice than to respond negatively. This is due to something that's popularly called vibes. It is your behavior that projects onto your partner. Your emotions are transferred onto him, and he doesn't have control over his emotions and behaviors. Seeing you in such negative light leaves him without options. He might be coping with his own insecurities, and to help you need to become the image of calmness, security and peace that you want to see in your relationship.

It is very difficult to change unhelpful behaviors because they become habits, and as any habits it is easy to go back to them. But now that you observed how those behaviors influence your partner and your relationship, you are aware that you need to change them. Focus on your values and the change will be much easier. Your values are what comes naturally to you. They are the morality that guides you through life. They are not something you think about; you feel them as part of you. You need to learn how to behave according to your values, not your emotions.

Do the Opposite

It will take a lot of energy to resist old habits and change your behavior to helpful ones, but as you practice and access new adopted behaviors, it will become easier. At one point, it will come without effort, almost automatically and naturally. This will make you feel better about yourself; it will be a great accomplishment. Instead of feeling unworthy, you will start to boost your self-esteem. Even your partner will recognize your effort and will reward you with even more love.

If you see and feel that all your previous behaviors didn't work, then it's only logical to do the opposite and see how that ends up. But what would the opposite be? First, let's look at some usual responses and behaviors you might have.

For example, you have abandonment insecurity and emotional deprivation core belief. You are dating your partner and you really like him. A situation happens at work that triggers your insecurities and you need reassurance; it's only natural to seek it from your partner. You call him, but he doesn't answer. You call him three more times to no avail. You start thinking that he doesn't like you as much as you like him; he is going to leave you, otherwise he would answer the phone. You start feeling anxious, depressed and scared, and you are already hurting. You have a strong urge to find out why isn't he answering right away and you keep calling. He finally answers the phone; he is in panic and asks what's wrong. You explain it's nothing, just your job and your need to hear his voice. He then informs you that he was in the middle of meeting with an important client and your constant calling disrupted it. He hangs up. You feel bad about the situation and text him asking for forgiveness and say you panicked, and it is not your usual behavior. But it is; it is the behavior pattern you have when you feel insecure. Soon enough, your partner will have enough and will want out of the relationship.

Now we can break down your behavior from the previously described experience and see how we can turn an unhelpful behavioral pattern into a helpful pattern.

1. You seek unnecessary communication.

2. You need reassurance.

3. You are clingy.

4. You are in need for certainty.

This would be helpful, opposite behavior:

1. Do not initiate communication and if you must, be sure you are not intruding on your partner's privacy.

2. Instead, pick up a distracting behavior. It can involve hobby, a quick exercise or simply organize your work desk.

3. Instead of thinking about yourself, do something for a colleague, volunteer, or walk a neighbor's dog. Be helpful to others, shift focus from yourself to someone else.

4. Be aware of situations that trigger your insecurity. Stay in the present and don't give into the traps of our minds. Meditate or have a relaxing cup of tea while contemplating a present experience.

Remember, you have insecurities coming from your different core beliefs. Your situation might be different, but the steps you need to take to overcome it are the same as shown in the example. Be sure to use your personal values as guidance for helpful behaviors. This way, you won't feel like you are going against your nature and it will be easier to master newly adopted behaviors.

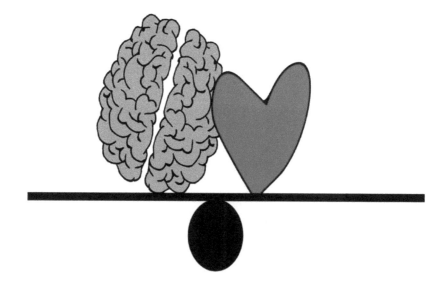

Chapter 9: Learn New Communication Skills

Now that you know how to manage your core beliefs, emotions and behaviors in a helpful way, it is time to learn how to communicate with your partner to ensure a healthy, long-lasting relationship.

Communication plays a very important role in building a successful and happy relationship. How many times did you hear the phrase "Communication is the key to happiness?" This phrase is true and soon enough, with practice, you will see why. Communication needs to be effective and it needs to allow us to connect with our partner. If you have poor communication skills, your relationship will most likely be unfulfilling and unhealthy. Communication is a skill that is learned, and you might have had bad role models during your childhood. Maybe your parents had bad communication skills and you learned from them. Your communication skills may get you a brief benefit, but in the long run, they may do more harm than good. With the change of harmful behaviors, you need to change poor communication skills to good ones and your relationship will bloom.

Remember that the behaviors you used to cope with insecurities are the things of past. When it comes to communication, you need to leave everything you know behind you, and be ready to learn and practice some new skills. In this chapter, you will find new communication skills that will help you build a connection with your partner and will help you avoid situations that might trigger your insecurities. The skills you will learn are self-disclosure and listening skills: expression of needs, validation skills, empathy, and apology.

Learn to Share

Self-disclosure is a communication skill that allows us to open ourselves to others. For some people, the thought of sharing personal information can be intimidating. We often have the perception that if we open ourselves to others, we will become vulnerable. Self-disclosure leaves us with unpleasant thoughts that are product of our insecurities.

"What if he leaves me when he gets to know the real me?" or "If he learns the truth about me, he will not love me anymore."

Feeling vulnerable in front of your partner is essential, however, make sure he or she is understanding towards your feelings. There are various behaviors that can trigger your insecurities, and you should seek to avoid them. There is also no need to be open towards absolutely everyone, only a select few. Keep in mind that trust is vital to a functional relationship, therefore both you and your partner should develop a bond of trust before openly sharing with one another. In addition, you need to find a balance between the information that you share with everyone, and that which you share only with your partner.

If you are constantly hiding behind a false image, you will never be able to achieve closeness with anyone; you are denying yourself a connection with your partner. There is no such thing as permanently removing triggers of insecurity. You need to learn how to manage them and being able to self-disclose might just be perfect manager of certain triggers.

When it comes to communication, self-disclosure is not only about words. Humans are capable of revealing information about themselves through facial expressions, body language, or our behavior. Some of these you are fully aware of and can control. Some you don't even notice, but others will. The trick is to be aware when and what is appropriate to communicate when insecurity triggers.

We could say we all have two parts: the *open self*, which is the image of your true self that you're comfortable with sharing, and the *hidden self*, the part you're uncomfortable sharing. What you need to do is tap into your *hidden self* and communicate about it to others. In other words, try to expand your *open self* and include to it some part of your *hidden self*. Your relationship can only benefit if you are able to disclose your feelings, thoughts, and needs… and your partner will appreciate your willingness to share.

How Much to Share

Each stage of a relationship can withstand different amounts of information being shared. On a first date, you won't reveal your deepest, darkest secrets about yourself. That would be off-putting and a bit pathological. As there is a time for self-disclosure, there is also a place. You won't tell your partner your experience with losing a friend/parent over a dinner date in a restaurant. During the relationship, there are stages you need to be aware to conclude how much information is too much. Let's have a look at those stages:

Stage 1: This is the early stage of relationship. You just started dating and to get to know each other. This is a good time to share information that includes your job, friends, and family... remember, you should share facts that include when, what, where, who or with who. You may share some interesting experiences you've had with your friends and family, but don't talk about your feelings and thoughts just yet. Your new partner should be comfortable to share the same amount and type of information. When you feel that the relationship might go forward and have a future, it is time to move on to step 2.

Step 2: You become able to share your thoughts and opinions, feelings and needs. It's important to keep the conversations all about past or future. Talk about your plans for the future to relocate or change your job. You may also want to share facts about your childhood, how you grew up with five sisters. When you feel the need to talk about your feelings and needs in present time, it is time for step 3.

Step 3: This is the step that most people with insecurities dread. It's time to share your feelings, thoughts, and needs. Step 3 carries the most risk as you will be vulnerable and expect the same from your partner. He needs to share the same or similar information so both of you will feel comfortable.

These steps are just guidance, you do not have to follow them strictly. Observe them and decide for yourself where your comfort level is for each. Self-disclosure is maybe a new skill for you, and you might need more practice before you learn where your comfort zone is. Take time and practice with your friends, parents, or partner.

Self-Disclosure is Rewarding

If you keep expanding your *open self*, referring to the things you want to share with your partner, there is a surprise for you. It's a rewarding feeling of getting to know yourself better. You will be surprised to see how opening to others will raise self-awareness. Hearing yourself talk aloud about your thoughts might give you insight into how you feel. For example, you've always thought you were too lazy and you came to this conclusion when you were 20 years old. Now, when you are in your mid-thirties, you say it out loud and it will start the process of dissecting your thoughts, analyzing and looking objectively, and you may conclude that your past thoughts aren't valid anymore. In the meantime, you became a worker bee but you never gave it a thought and you continued considering yourself lazy. Now you possess a new knowledge about yourself, and this is the reward for your self-disclosure.

Another reward is having a close relationship with your partner. If you and your partner engage in self-disclosure, you will come to respect each other more. The bond between you will become stronger from the knowledge that you trust each other enough to share your private thoughts and feelings. Without mutual self-disclosure, your relationship will become unsatisfying and won't last. It is also unsatisfying if only one side shares information about themselves. It can trigger insecurities, and this is why you need to be aware that for self-closure there are times and places. In some situations, your partner might feel uncomfortable to open up so don't push. Self-disclosure needs to come naturally in a safe space such as your shared home.

Self-disclosure is also a good way to earn your partner's trust. If you are comfortable sharing information about yourself, he or she will come to the conclusion that he can do the same. In a way, by disclosing yourself, you are encouraging your partner to do the same. This will lead to better communication and a healthier relationship.

Being able to talk about yourself and your past experiences, thoughts, and emotions will lessen any feelings of guilt or shame you might feel. By saying some of it out loud, you will come to the conclusion that your experiences are not unique and that there is no need to carry the burden alone.

Learn to Listen

If you want to build healthy communication skills, listening is essential. It will only help you build a long-lasting, happy relationship. When you feel you are being heard, you feel empowered. It will give you a boost to share even more because other people will show they care. They'll acknowledge what you say and validate you. You need to do the same to validate your partner. Listening must go both ways; there can't be only one side listening. This will make one of you feel unappreciated and will disconnect you. The relationship will suffer.

Before we learn how to listen, let's look at the reasons why we don't listen. It could be because of distractions or the inability to focus. We all experience these barriers and we need to overcome them to be able to learn active listening.

You've probably experienced half-listening before. You can recognize it in yourself and in others as well. For example, you are talking to your partner and mid-story, you say something that you know your partner will respond to. You might even ask him a question. But he remains silent, looking at you as if he is listening but the lack of response is an obvious sign he's not focused on your story. He will even be capable of repeating what you said word for word, but it is clear that he didn't process all the information you gave him. You've probably been guilty of half-listening yourself. This happens because our focus is split on the story we are listening to, and our thoughts that are constantly popping. They can be related to the story but might also be completely unrelated and even more distracting. It is easy to notice when you start half-listening, and you can force yourself back on track. Deny your thoughts access to your consciousness and concentrate on your partner's story.

There are different types of blocks we encounter when we should be carefully listening. They are easy to overcome with some extra focus, but you won't notice if you don't become aware of them. So, let's list some.

1. **Comparing**: This usually happens when we listen to our partner talk, but we constantly compare his experience with our own. This block is common with people who have insecurities.

2. **Mind reading**: It happens when the one who listens tries to predict what the speaker will say next or tries to figure out what the speaker really means or feels.

3. **Rehearsing**: This happens when the one who is supposed to be listening is obsessed with what he will respond to the speaker, or if he is next to talk.

4. **Filtering**: If we find particular subject unpleasant, we can often catch our mind wandering and not be prepared to listen the unpleasant story.

5. **Dreaming**: Simply put, the listener is daydreaming and not paying attention to the speaker.

6. **Identifying**: The listener often interrupts the speaker to share his experience with the particular subject.

7. **Advising**: The listener interrupts the speaker with the advice he or she has to offer even before speaker is done with his story.

8. **Sparring**: This happens when the listener is interrupting the speaker to disagree or to debate.

9. **Being right**: This happens when the listener is not allowing the speaker to prove him wrong.

10. **Derailing**: The listener, for one reason or another, changes the subject.

11. **Placating**: The listener is more focused on being supportive and sounding nice than actually listening.

We all have listening blocks, some of them we are aware of and some we aren't. Listening blocks are the bad habits that will hold our relationship back. We need to get rid of these bad habits if we want to build a healthy, long-lasting relationship. Which of the listening blocks listed above do you recognize in yourself? It can be more than one depending on the situation and the person who is speaking. Think of your partner, you probably know what in his tone triggers one of these listening blocks. For a happy relationship, it is of great importance to be open but not just about yourself. You also need to be open about the things your partner is telling you.

If you have abandonment or failure insecurities and your partner tells you "We need to talk" you will probably use a *filtering* block, so you don't hear the bad things he or she has to say. But what if you are missing something important? Something you can acknowledge and easily change to make your relationship better. Don't dismiss your partner so easily; be open-minded about what he has to say.

Learn Active Listening

Now that you are aware of your own listening blocks, you are ready to engage the conversation process and listen to your partner. Active listening means you are able to respond to your partner's stories not just with words, but with body language and facial expressions. This will not only tell your reactions; it will also indicate that you are truly listening. As a person with relationship insecurities, there are things available for you to help you not just be better listener but to learn more about your insecurities, and you will see them clearly for what they are:

Paraphrasing: When dealing with insecurities, it is very important to paraphrase what your partner is saying. This will leave no space for miscommunication and you will clearly know what your partner is communicating. Paraphrasing is useful for remembering conversations and, later, if you bring it up there will be no misunderstandings.

Clarifying: It is more an extension of paraphrasing, but it means you will ask questions to make certain you understand your partner. You will get more information by doing so, and you will be able to fill any gaps you had in understanding. It will also let your partner know you are actively communicating with him or her.

Feedback: Simply respond to your partner's story. You can even talk about how their story influenced you and how it made you feel. Giving feedback is a great opportunity to open up and be honest with your partner. But be sure to ask your partner how he feels about his story. You might have the understanding of his thoughts, but you are still uncertain of how he feels. Don't shy away from asking questions when you are giving feedback.

Learn How to Express Your Needs

Expressing your needs may be very challenging especially if you don't possess that skill. Insecure people often have problem saying out loud what they want, and they act submissively to please their partner so they don't trigger their insecurities. Many convince themselves that they have no needs, and they are satisfied with fulfilling their partner's needs. Insecure people think if they express their needs, they will be rejected or they will be left behind or even be abandoned.

The truth is, we all live with the knowledge that not all of our needs are going to be met. It all boils down to how much you allow your unmet needs to affect you. To communicate your needs you need to be realistic about them and assess the situation. You won't express the need for constant reassurance at the beginning of your relationship. It will scare away your potential partner. Be smart about it, see where your relationship is in the present, how much you and your partner trust each other and then decide if he is able to meet your needs. If he can't meet your needs, that doesn't mean he will never be. Don't hesitate to express the need. Just lower your expectations and be prepared to feel some pain. It will motivate your partner to go forward and so he can meet your needs sometime in the future.

There are some points you should follow when expressing your needs. This way you will avoid any misunderstandings:

1. Don't blame your partner or put a fault on him. ("I need you to

not be so cold with me.")

2. Don't be judgmental when expressing your need. ("I need you to be less stubborn.")

3. Make sure you give clear and understandable information about your needs. ("I need you to hug me" instead of "I need you to show more affection.")

4. Don't ask for more than one need at the time as this will only lead to confusion.

Remember, not all your needs will be met but the way you express them will eliminate any possible miscommunication and it will hurt less if your need is denied. With proper communication, your partner will give explanation why at this moment he or she cannot meet your needs. Our loved ones always want to please us and want to meet our needs, although not always possible.

Learn How and What to Validate

Validation is an important part of communication. It doesn't mean you are agreeing or disagreeing with your partner's story. It means you are acknowledging his experience and you accept it as genuine. When your partner tells you the story, his thoughts and feelings, it is important for him to feel validated because everything less than that will make him feel hurt, judged, or abandoned. Validation has a soothing effect on people and builds trust and connection.

Validation makes a statement real. For example, if your partner tells you he's insecure, instead of saying, "There's nothing to be insecure about" try saying, "I can see you are insecure." This will not only let him know you are aware of his emotions and thoughts, it will also reinforce him to continue opening himself to you, thus bringing him closer to dealing with his insecurities. If your partner is overreacting or underreacting to some situation that triggers his insecurities, you may want to validate those insecurities. If your partner is connecting your anger to abuse because of childhood experiences, you need to validate his reaction and say, "I can understand why you think I will hurt you…" and continue reassuring him you won't. Don't forget to put yourself in your partner's shoes. Validate his reactions not just by showing you understand, make him feel part of a group. Say things like, "I would react the same as you if that happened to me." This is a powerful way of validating because it also means we approve and it gives reassurance. Do it only if your partner's reaction to a situation was positive and healthy. Approving negative behavior will not lead to healthier relationship.

You also have to know what exactly to validate. Be sure to validate emotions, even the negative ones. Validating positive emotions is empowering and will make your partner feel good about himself. It will reassure him. Validating negative emotions will sooth him and will lessen the impact of those emotions and make the pain less intensive.

Validate your partner's wishes and desires. That doesn't mean you have to fulfill them, not that your partner wants you to. It simply means you are there to support your partner and acknowledge what he wants. Give him strength to achieve what he intended. When your partner talks about his wishes and desires, he might be opening himself to you on a more personal level. Be aware if you don't validate him at this point, it might lead to him closing up again and going back to feeling insecure.

Always validate his beliefs and opinions, even if you do not agree with them. Validating beliefs and opinions means you respect your partner and accept him for what he is.

Validate your partners actions, make sure you don't approve of negative actions, but you can still acknowledge them with validation, it will show that you care.

Validate suffering. Understanding one's pain means that you understand him, care and accept him. It also means you are there for him.

Learn Empathy

Empathy builds deep connections with your partner. We all have some negative experiences in our past, and we all carry some deep pains from those times. It might manifest itself into insecurity, or it may not, but in any case the pain is still there. Because of this, it is important to regard your partner as a person who carries pain and is struggling with it. The experiences are different, and you might not agree with the way your partner chooses to deal with his pain, but you can understand it. Understanding means connecting with your partner's experience even though you don't share it.

Empathy means compassion, and we can offer it only when we truly understand our partner's pain. Empathy brings us closer to our partner; it truly builds a bridge between two individuals.

Cognitive empathy is our ability to understand other people's emotions without feeling them ourselves. You may understand that your partner is frustrated by a situation at work, but you don't feel it yourself. In that case you will say, "I see how that must be frustrating." Cognitive empathy is similar to validation and is an important part of communication if you want to build a happy relationship. Words are not always needed to show that we understand. In frustrating situations, show compassion by hugging. Don't try to break the frustration with humor. It will show that you can't be bothered to deal with your partner's emotions.

Emotional empathy is when we do feel exactly what our partner is feeling. When your partner is happy because of something, you don't just feel good for him, you feel happy with him.

Enhance your Empathy

In order to enhance your empathy, you have to remove anything that is in your way of natural expression of empathy. It can be various things such as listening blocks, not being focused, or distractions from the outside.

One of the biggest obstacles of showing empathy is being overly concerned with how we feel instead of our partner. This means we don't see the situation from our partners point of view; we're rather obsessed with how the situation affects us. If you notice your thoughts are wandering toward your inner self, and you are concerned about yourself more than for your partner, take a break in the conversation. Give yourself time to cool off and return to conversation when you become aware that the communication you are having with your partner is about him and his experience. This doesn't mean you are not allowed to feel for yourself, just that it's not a good time to be selfish; your partner needs you now.

Give your partner all of your attention. Attention means you are giving your best to understand your partner. Only once you completely understand what he or she is going through will you be able to show true empathy. Yes, empathy can be faked, but your partner will feel it isn't genuine and it can hurt your relationship even more. Subtle signs such as the tone of your voice, facial expressions and body language will make your partner feel more betrayed by a faked attempt at empathy.

To make sure you can be empathetic, stop wondering what's best for your partner and stop thinking you can help him. At this point, that is irrelevant. Your partner needs empathy, problem solving can come once you've showed you care and feel for him. The urge to immediately help is strong, especially when we see them suffering, but showing empathy means creating connection with your partner, making your partner trust you so he can allow you to help. People who are insecure in a relationship often lack this trust, and empathy is a great way of building it. Humans are prone to quickly connecting to people who understand them, and empathy is understanding.

Learn to Apologize

We are often unaware of how our actions and words influence our partner. It may come to you as a surprise that something you said in a jokingly manner hurt or insulted your partner. You caused the pain without intending to. The pain is there, and your partner needs to deal with it. To help, it's a good idea to apologize. An apology will ease your partner's pain, and it will bring understanding and a deeper connection.

Many people don't have a habit of apologizing, and this might be because parents sometimes don't apologize to children. In the past, when it comes to the relationship between parent and child, apologies were regarded as a sign of weakness and loss of authority. Modern parenting shies away from these thoughts and apologizing to your children becomes a more natural act. Even adults are sometimes wrong, and if we as adults apologize, we will teach our children how to do it and when to do it. Insecure people might have trouble apologizing and it can be a sign of failure core beliefs. Such people don't like to apologize thinking it will put a light on their inadequacy.

How you word your apology is the most important part of it. It must be sincere, but it also must be clear and easy to understand. An apology must convince your partner that you are taking responsibility for your words or actions that caused him pain. Don't say, "I'm sorry your feelings are hurt," say something like "I'm sorry my words hurt your feelings." Do you see the difference? In the first apology, we are accusing our partner of being easy to hurt. We accuse him of the way he perceives our words. In the second, we are sincerely sorry to cause him pain. Knowing how to apologize is a very important communication skill, and it takes practice. We are all prone to reacting impulsively, especially if we are having an argument with a loved one. Make sure you are rational and cool-headed before you apologize. Make sure your partner is not emotionally elevated. Take time before apologizing, no matter when it comes. If it's sincere, an apology is always received in a positive way.

All the communication skills we listed above will help you build strong, meaningful relationships. Practice communication whenever you have the chance. It doesn't matter if you are the one with the insecurity in your relationship or your partner, communication needs to be healthy on both sides. Communication skills best work when they can rely on each other. An apology is best accepted if it's filled with empathy, and for best results combine listening with validation. Communication is not an easy skill to master, and you'll need a lot of practice. Try these skills with your family and friends, practice whenever there is a chance. The most important communication skill is being aware when you make mistakes and correcting them immediately. Stop, don't rush. Listen to your own words before you articulate them. Try to predict how they will influence your partner and adjust them accordingly. Every effort toward healthier communication will be noticed by your partner, and he will put forth the same effort.

Chapter 10: Build a Healthy, Long-Lasting and Loving Relationship

In the previous chapters, you learned how to deal with your insecurities or how to manage your partner's. You also learned where they come from and how to communicate about them. But there is more the relationship, especially if you want to build a strong one.

All relationships need nurturing. You and your partner need to be able to walk together through life. This can be achieved only if you trust each other and you know how to communicate effectively. Even when your relationship is at its worst, to be able to survive, you both need to invest in it. But relationships also need you to understand that you and your partner are separate individuals that have their own differences. Never try to change your partner. Relationship means compromise.

Change Naturally

We all do change through our lives due to new experiences, and we can't be the same person we were before this relationship. But that kind of change is natural, and people don't even notice it. But don't force the change, don't insist on it and don't expect it in your partner. Observe the ones that happen to you, they are important lessons and they need to make us better person. For example, before you met your partner you never really gave a thought about exercising. Your partner loves to hike and to spend more time with him you decide to join him. This new activity you share with your partner made you realize how your body is changing for the better, you come to conclusion that your health improved due to hiking, and you decide to give even more to it. You start going to the gym every now and then and you take care of yourself more. This is influencing you; you changed something about yourself in a positive way, and it is making both you and your partner happy. This is an example of good change that happened naturally and it came from an experience. The forced change would be your partner making you go hike with him even if you don't want to. He forces you to go to the gym by conditioning you with various things. You don't like it, but you feel obligated to do it for your partner. Given enough time, your insecurities will trigger and you will start arguing about it. After all, you are doing something you don't want to. It will build anxiety between you and the relationship will suffer.

Keep the Connection Alive

Partners drift away from each other sometimes due to everyday stresses. It can be related to work, family, or friends. Our attachment styles, the same ones that cause insecurities, may give us an early warning and we have the advantage of having the time to react and work on reconnecting with our partner. Keeping the connection you and your partner built requires work. There are things you can do so you don't allow your relationship to suffer from loss of connection:

Set a daily ritual. At the end of the day, spend some time with your partner talking about the experiences you had that day. Listen how your partner spent his day and get involved by asking questions. Be an active listener and ask how he felt. If they were bad, show compassion and affection. Tell him about your day, what you did or who you met. Talk about your family and shared friends. If you don't feel like doing this, consider making plans with your partners for the future. Spend time just the two of you and share ideas about the future. It can be individual things you want to do or something you want to share with your partner. Conversations at the end of the day often provide support and a feeling of coming back to something secure, your relationship. It will help you to share through difficult times or share your happy times. There is no need to spend specific time talking, do it as long as you feel comfortable but do it every day. The routine of these conversations will leave you with the feeling that there is something to be happy about at the end of the day, and there is security at home.

Spend quality time together. This is about experiencing the same thing together. Without this part, the relationship might not exist. Couples do get caught up in their personal lives and they do forget that they need to spend more quality time with their partner to be happy. We live in an age when we have to work most of our time, and we work when we are home. Instead of spending our free time for ourselves and our partner, we often use it to catch up with work or school. It is important to spend quality time with your partner. It can be going to a concert, dinner date, enjoying a sport together, or having a movie night. It is not enough if your partner is next to you and your attention is on your work. That is not quality time. It's just being in the same room. Remember how exciting it was at the beginning of your relationship to spend each moment of the day together? You can relive those times if you give yourself a bit of time to share activities with your partner.

Share a project. Many couples say that the best spent quality time with their partner is when they shared a task. From repainting the house and playing together with your children, volunteering together for the same cause, couples find it helpful to reconnect if they have a common goal. Working together on a project will reveal the true meaning of the word "partners" and it will shed light on how to plan your life together, how to communicate better and how to focus on each other. It is a great way of combining obligations and quality time.

Show Love through Actions

In a relationship, both you and your partner do nice things for each other. But couples often take each other for granted, especially later in the relationship when it matures. When this happens, they feel disconnected, lonely and even rejected.

When there is a lack of affectionate actions in the beginning of the relationship, you might need to ask yourself if he or she is really the one for you. Is the attraction going both ways or are you the only one who is interested? Maybe it's just your insecurities of rejection or failure that make you want to continue seeing this person or maybe he is triggering your insecurities and your attachment style keeps you feeling affection for your partner.

Some people expect from their partners to know what will make them happy and believe that if there is a need to say out loud what you want. It invalidates the action their partner took to please them. But is it really fair to expect your partner to read your mind? Nobody can know you that well to be able to predict things about you. You have to ask yourself is the action really more important than your partners intention to make you happy? After all, if you are obsessing about the action itself, or the gift itself, you are completely missing the point of relationship. Show off your newly learned communication skills in situations like these. Be mindful and tell your partner openly what would make you happy. You can even ask for it, just be smart about it. Instead of saying, "I want you to buy me this painting for my birthday," say something like, "You know, my birthday is getting close and I saw this really amazing painting…" It's a hint nobody can miss. It is obvious what you want, yet you are leaving space for your partner to think about it and maybe come with his own idea that will surprise you.

Be Honest

Trust and honesty are very important key ingredients for successful relationship. They are also probably the most difficult to maintain. It takes hard work from both you and your partner to be able to maintain them and keep your relationship from falling apart. There are guides on how to keep the honesty in relationship to a satisfying level, and both you and your partner need to follow so you can make each other happy.

Promote honesty. It is essential in building a healthy relationship. Attraction and love were just the components that made the relationship happen, what will keep it going and make it last is honesty. Forget about little white lies you've been practicing with your previous partners or friends and family. If you want this relationship to really work, be completely honest. We use white lies mainly to make our partner feel better or happy, but if he or she finds out the truth, it may crush them, trigger their own insecurities and make them not believe you in future.

Detect dishonesty. Use your intuition to detect if someone is lying to you. Intuition is a great weapon and it works in our favor. Observe body language, facial expressions and intonation of a person if you suspect he is lying to you. If you catch your partner in lie, don't be dramatic about it. Maybe he's just not aware how much truth means to you. Don't start quarrels and arguments, use your communication skills to let them know you are aware of the lie, and how much it would mean to you to know the truth. Let them know you understand why they might think lying is the right option, but also make clear that you value the truth even if it hurts you. Our loved ones lie to us with good intentions, they want us to avoid feeling pain or they think it is acceptable to tell a small lie to make us feel happy. Let them know this is wrong and show them by example how much you value truth.

Be emotionally honest. You need to stop with closing your emotions away. Learn how to express them and most of all, be honest about them

116

to yourself. There is no benefit of avoiding emotions, lying yourself about them. If you are unable to acknowledge them, how do you expect your partner to do so? How do you expect him to behave in your relationship if he is unsure of how you feel? Take time to think about your emotions, acknowledge them for what they are and then talk about them with your partner. To practice "the emotion talk" start with simple stuff. Don't just tell your partner what you did today, also tell him how you felt about things you did.

Don't keep secrets. Unless they are birthday surprises, Christmas presents, or just surprise affection acts. Those are safe to keep. Anything else can lead to your partner not trusting you anymore. It is same as with white lies; keeping secret might hurt your partner and start the downfall of your relationship. Most people find out if the partner kept a secret so what's the point? Avoid any uncomfortable situations and see that it's only beneficial for your relationship if you don't keep secrets from your partner.

Once the trust is broken, it takes building up the relationship from the beginning to gain it back. It is a very difficult and long process, but it can be done. Communicate with your partner what went wrong and why was the trust broken. Only through understanding can you move on. Don't just shrug it off because it will return and bite you. Broken trust is the number one reason for a breakup. The key to rebuilding trust is to live in the present. If you made peace with the fact that your partner lied to you, don't think he will always lie. Don't evaluate all of his actions to see if he is being truthful. That means you are not able to let go. Observe his actions in present and don't associate them with past lies. Trust yourself to be able to detect if he is being untruthful, don't go above and beyond searching for lies. If you are the one who committed the lie, there is no action that will prove your honesty to your partner. There is nothing you can do to convince him or her that you will never do it again. Such a promise is a heavy one, and what if you can't fulfill it? Let your partner regain your trust in time in his own way. The only thing you can do is practice honesty at all times. Don't give in to old habits, be truthful and considerate. Your partner will see your good intentions and will accept your honesty again.

Chapter 11: Quick Tips for New Relationships

You should view this chapter as a continuation of your journey toward increased self-love, self-determination, and compassion. Whether you're already in a relationship, or just getting into one, you should bring hopeful but realistic expectations regarding what you can achieve. Use them to learn more about yourself and practice everything you've learned so far in order to improve your love life.

Other's Core Beliefs

While it's important to be aware of yourself and your behavior, you should also make room to extend the same awareness to someone else. When you spend some time with someone, you will gain enough information to gain an insight into his or her beliefs. Keep in mind that core beliefs aren't the issue. It's all about the way a person responds to them and the resulting behavior. Your partner's behavior (or your date's behavior) can significantly impact the way you view yourself.

Certain behaviors are tolerable and you may consider accepting them even if they cause discomfort, to a certain degree. Depending on how new the relationship is, however, you may have to wait for these behaviors to come to light. You need to take your time and see whether the person you are with exhibits unpredictable behavior patterns or is highly reliable. During the early stages of a relationship your insecurities, or anxiety, may cause you issues due to the uncertainties you are facing. You need to be mindful and self-aware about your own feelings and behavior. However, there are certain behavior patterns that you may deem undesirable or unacceptable:

1.   **Unpredictable**: Your partner (date) changes or cancels plans suddenly without giving you any time to adjust to the new information. He or she may also make communication difficult because of unpredictable changes in his or her thought process. Keep in mind that someone with an unpredictable behavior can seem highly attractive because this type of person is often interesting and fun to be around when he eventually shows up. However, the constant uncertainty will keep you emotionally confused.

2.   **Unstable**: Your partner has a habit of making important life changes frequently. This type of person often moves around and changes friends, as well as jobs, at a high rate. He has the ability to move and adapt without any consequences. This is someone you may find attractive because of the carefree, relaxed attitude. However, the lack of stability is not something you may be able to cope with for extended periods of time.

3.   **Unavailable**: The time you spend with your partner is amazing and you couldn't be happier. He engages you emotionally, he provokes your inner thoughts and fulfills your days like no other person. However, he often disappears without a word of warning and you stop hearing from him for days at a time. This kind of person is unstable and will never be able to offer the security you need.

It isn't difficult to break-up with someone when you don't have a good time together. However, the situation is far more complex when you do occasionally have wonderful experiences. This is why you need to be aware of your own feelings whenever you are engaged in an activity with your date or partner. Take note of your emotions, observations and inner thoughts. If you keep track of them, you will have an easier time determining whether that person is right for you or not.

Warning Signs

Sometimes we are attracted to certain people because of the familiar behaviors they exhibit. Even if they are negative and we are aware of their damaging effects, we still sometimes choose to ignore them. Here are a number of unhealthy personality traits and behaviors you might be attracted to:

1.   **The judge:** This type of person thinks only in black and white concepts. Everything belongs to one extreme or the other, and he doesn't accept any other opinions other than his own.

2.   **The victim**: Things always happen to him and it's never his fault. He tends to be passive and often complains that others take advantage of him. He blames others for his problems and given enough time he will start placing the blame on you once the relationship matures.

3.   **The joker**: He may seem funny at times, however he hides his true face. He takes advantage of his developed sense of humor to mask his true

feelings about other people.

4.   **The critic**: This person will always find something wrong with you or with a situation. He is never satisfied under any circumstance and will often make you feel as if he is constantly searching for a new target to criticize.

5.   **The possessor**: A person who is in constant need of your attention. He will easily become angry and jealous of any other relationship you have, whether it's with your parents, friends, or coworkers. He is possessive and wants you to focus on him alone.

6.   **The catastrophizer**: This person will always view any negative event as a catastrophe. He tends to overreact often under any unfamiliar circumstances or when something doesn't go according to plan. He views everything from a negative point of view, making a healthy relationship nearly impossible.

Make sure to take note of any of these personality traits and behaviors whenever you notice them. It is easy to write them off as a one-time occurrence, however they can be the sign of a behavioral pattern.

Another's Values

We discussed earlier about the importance of identifying and developing your core values. However, it is equally important that the person you are with shares some of these values, although you don't have to be a perfect match.

Obviously, when your relationship is still new, or you are still going through the first dates, you can't just ask someone to list his personal values. Luckily, through communication you can gain enough information to make a fairly accurate guess. For example, if he's doing some charitable work like volunteering at an animal shelter you'll know that he is a caring and loving person.

You can use your journal to list both of your values, and his values in two side by side columns. Keep in mind that when you enter a new relationship everything tends to be exciting and you can easily forget about your own values, or you temporarily modify them to better match your partner. This kind of behavior can make you ignore the signs that should convey jealousy, possessiveness and other negative traits. This is one of the biggest challenges you may face in a new relationship. There is no certainty and your insecurities can easily creep up on you, even when you have made plenty of progress.

Conclusion

You now have all the knowledge you need to continue the battle with your insecurities. Your old behaviors and reactions weren't helpful and they made the situation even worse, but this time you will notice success because you will change your behavior. You learned how to deal with emotions and negative thoughts. You learned how to change your behavior so it doesn't hurt your relationship anymore. But this is only the beginning. It is the theoretical knowledge you need in order to understand where your insecurities are coming from and how to manage them.

You kept your own journal, and now you can refer to it whenever you feel the need. Read up what you wrote about the attachment styles you recognized within yourself. Refer to core beliefs and keep practicing positive behaviors. Be sure you are on the right path to improving the quality of your relationship. Notice how your partner is changing his own behavior in response and how positively it affects both of you and your relationship.

Now you know how to stay motivated, and even though you are aware you cannot control your core beliefs, emotions or negative thoughts, you have the power to keep your reactions helpful so they benefit your relationship.

Keep practicing your communication skills. You probably already started noticing how communication is important for building a healthy and strong relationship. Your partner might need some knowledge of positive communication too, help him learn it, set the example. Practice validation and empathy together.

Above all, love your partner. Without love, there is no relationship, so don't forget to show it through actions and words. Spend quality time with your partner. Unfortunately, the modern age doesn't leave us with much free time. Invest in your relationship and be prepared to give, to be open and to reconnect with your partner.

This book might seem overwhelming at times, so do not rush it. You will not learn anything useful that way. Give it time and return to it when needed. It is unrealistic to expect to be free of insecurities, but after reading this book just once, you will feel the improvement. To completely regain the feeling of security, return to this book as many times as you have to. Don't be shy to ask for help and be brave on the journey of conquering your insecurities.

Bibliography

Becker-Phelps, L. (2016). Insecure in love: How anxious attachment can make you feel jealous, needy, and worried and what you can do about it. New Harbinger Publications

Gunther, R. (2010). Relationship saboteurs: Overcoming the ten behaviors that undermine love. Oakland, CA: New Harbinger Publications.

Leahy, R. L. (2018). Jealousy Cure: Learn to Trust, Overcome Possessiveness, and Save Your Relationship. New Harbinger Publications.

Levine, A. (2012). Attached: The New Science of Adult Attachment and How It Can Help You Find - And Keep - Love. TarcherPerigee

Thieda, K. N. (2013). Loving someone with anxiety: Understanding & helping your partner.

CPSIA information can be obtained
at www.ICGtesting.com
Printed in the USA
BVHW011426031221
623078BV00002BA/11